W9-AYQ-485

Beyond
Douglass

Aperçus: *Histories Texts Cultures*

a Bucknell series

Series Editor: Greg Clingham

Aperçu (apersü). 1882. [Fr.] A *summary exposition, a conspectus.*

Relations among historiography, culture, and textual representation are presently complex and rich in possibilities. *Aperçus* is a series of books exploring the connections between these crucial terms. Revisionist in intention, *Aperçus* seeks to open up new possibilities for humanistic knowledge and study, and thus to deepen and extend our understanding of what history, culture, and texts have been and are, as these terms are made to bear on each other by new thinking and writing.

Titles in the Series

Critical Pasts: Writing Criticism, Writing History
ed. Philip Smallwood

History and Nation
ed. Julia Rudolph

Europe Observed: Multiple Gazes in Early Modern Encounters
ed. Kumkum Chatterjee and Clement Hawes

Beyond Douglass: New Perspectives on Early African-American Literature
ed. Michael J. Drexler and Ed White.

Beyond Douglass

New Perspectives on Early African-American Literature

WITHDRAWN
FROM THE
CARL B. YLVISAKER LIBRARY
Concordia College, Moorhead, MN

Edited by
Michael J. Drexler
and Ed White

Carl B. Ylvisaker Library
Concordia College
Moorhead. MN 56562

Lewisburg: Bucknell University Press

© 2008 by Rosemont Publishing & Printing Corp.

All rights reserved. Authorization to photocopy items for internal or personal use, or internal or personal use of specific clients, is granted by the copyright owner, provided that a base fee of $10.00, plus eight cents per page, per copy is paid directly to the Copyright Clearance Center, 222 Rosewood Drive, Danvers, Massachusetts 01923. [978-0-8387-5711-6/08 $10.00 + 8¢ pp, pc.]

Associated University Presses
2010 Eastpark Boulevard
Cranbury, NJ 08512

The paper used in this publication meets the requirements of the American National Standard
for Permanence of Paper for Printed Library Materials
Z39.48-1984.

Library of Congress Cataloging-in-Publication Data

Beyond Douglass : new perspectives on early African-American literature / edited by
Michael J. Drexler and Ed White.
        p.   cm.—(Aperçus)
    Includes bibliographical references and index.
    ISBN 978-0-8387-5711-6 (alk. paper)
    1. American literature—African American authors—History and criticism.   2. American
literature—African American authors—Study and teaching.   3. American literature—
Colonial period, ca. 1600–1775—History and criticism.   4. American literature—
Revolutionary period, 1775–1783—History and criticism.   5. American literature—19th
century—History and criticism.   6. American literature—1783–1850—History and
criticism.   7. Slaves' writings, American—History and criticism.   8. Autobiography—
African American authors.   9. African American—Intellectual life—18th century.
10. African Americans—Intellectual life—19th century.   I. Drexler, Michael J.
II. White, Ed, 1965–   III. Title.   IV. Series.

PS153.N5B49 2008
810.9′896073—dc22

                                                                                2008002293

PRINTED IN THE UNITED STATES OF AMERICA

Contents

Acknowledgments

WE OWE FIRST THANKS TO BUCKNELL UNIVERSITY PRESS EDITOR Greg Clingham for his support. Thanks to Camden House for permission to reprint Katherine Faull's essay, "Self-Encounters: Two Eighteenth-Century Memoirs from Moravian Bethlehem," which first appeared in *Crosscurrents: African Americans, Africa, and Germany in the Modern World*, edited by David McBride, Leroy Hopkins, and C. Aisha Blackshire-Belay (Columbia, SC: Camden House, 1998). We also wish to thank Kimberley Drexler, John Enyeart, Robin Jacobson, Scott Meinke, and Janice Traflet. Thanks also to Amisha Sharma, Julie Kim, Jodi Schorb, Leah Rosenberg, and Trysh Travis.

*   *   *   *

Katherine Faull's essay is dedicated to the memory of Emmanuel Chukwudi Eze (1963–2007). Faull writes, "Andrew and Magdalene's stories delimited the beginning and the end of ours. But now they will be retold."

Beyond Douglass

Michael J. Drexler and Ed White

Canon Loading

IN THE PAST TWO DECADES, A CANON OF BLACK WRITING HAS emerged to become codified in any number of American literature anthologies. This canon extends from a cluster of late eighteenth-century writers—above all Olaudah Equiano and Phillis Wheatley—and culminates in the writings of Frederick Douglass and Harriet Jacobs. Between these poles one finds a fairly consistent constellation of secondary figures—David Walker, Henry Highland Garnet, Nat Turner, William Wells Brown, and Martin Delany—but attention seems focused on the two poles of origin and fulfillment, foundation and cap-stone. Meanwhile, in contrast to the steady persistence of this canon, the past decade has witnessed the continued valuable scholarship of recla-mation evident in a number of important collections: Vincent Carretta's *Unchained Voices: An Anthology of Black Authors in the English-Speaking World of the Eighteenth Century* (1996); Robert J. Cottrol's *From African to Yankee: Narratives of Slavery and Freedom in Antebellum New England* (1998); Yuval Taylor's two-volume anthology of slave narratives, *I Was Born a Slave* (1999); the Library of America's new volume of *Slave Narratives* (ed. W. Andrews and H. L. Gates, 2000); *Pamphlets of Protest: An Anthology of Early African-American Protest Literature, 1790–1860* (ed. R. Newman, P. Rael, and P. Lapsansky, 2001); *"Face Zion Forward": First*

Writers of the Black Atlantic, 1785–1798 (ed. J. Brooks and J. Saillant, 2002); William L. Andrews's anthologies of *Classic African American Women's Narratives* (2003) and *North Carolina Slave Narratives* (2003); and Robert S. Levine's *Martin Delany: A Documentary Reader* (2003).

Judging from other cycles of canon expansion, whether that led by feminists or the attempt to include a Native American presence, we might speculate that these more recently reclaimed works will remain texts for the specialist and will neither enter nor significantly modify the newly established canon. This is more than a historical and analytical problem of improved understanding, for while this simplified and truncated canon may seem to some a quantitative matter (there are only so many pages in an anthology, only so much time can be granted African-American writers, etc.), it more profoundly betrays a pedagogic desire for a unified national story of heroic writer figures, with a concomitant set of fixed problematizations. Put more simply, the teaching canon serves a function at times opposed to our very goals in the classroom, privileging representative extremes over nuanced complications. This reified use of the early African-American canon becomes clearer when we examine the semiotic system anchored by two pairs of writers: Olaudah Equiano and Phillis Wheatley in the late eighteenth century, and Frederick Douglass and Harriet Jacobs on the eve of the Civil War. Equiano and Douglass each signal the articulation of an ostensibly typical and predictive African-American subjectivity, with the transition from the former to the latter essentially tracing a series of changes characteristic of the more traditional canon. Thus the common shorthand narrative traces a shift akin to that from Jonathan Edwards to Benjamin Franklin, here the move from Equiano's religiously charged language and more limited social engagement (e.g., the narrower definition of abolition), to Douglass's more secular and patriotic subjectivity, for which politics (now an expanded sense of abolition) is itself the sign of a broader program of consciousness-raising and national (or racial) pride. The assumption of this narrativized canon, of course, is that Douglass is something of an archetype, a position influentially articulated two decades ago in James Olney's essay " 'I Was Born': Slave Narratives, Their Status as Autobiography and as Literature." There Olney insisted that the reader of slave narratives "is sure to come away dazed by the mere repetitiveness of it all" (46), before asserting that Douglass's *Narrative of the Life of Frederick Douglass* . . . was "at once the best example, the exceptional case, and the supreme achievement" (54).[1] Accordingly, any number of texts, slave narratives or otherwise, represent this gradual move toward the exemplar. Intermediate narratives are fine-tunings on the way to Douglass, while Garnett's 1843 address or Walker's "Appeal" is to be read as a public and collective manifestation of a "protest" consciousness more richly accessible in the autobiographical mode.

Alongside these patriarchal poles, however, stand two necessary supplements. At the originary point, Phillis Wheatley's poetry becomes the epitome of the frustrations and limitations of engagement with a Euro-American tradition of writing, signaling either the tremendous obstacles and subsequent failings of the early Black writer or the inaugural gestures of signifying against the "white" literary tradition. At the other end of the timeline, Jacobs becomes the bridge figure between antebellum white women and the Douglass trunk, and thus a crucial moment of feminist critique of a by-now-distinctive African-American tradition. The status of the women, then, is all too apparent: they are variants or complications of their male counterparts, as if, in a critical division of labor, Equiano and Douglass assured the integrity and autonomy of the tradition while Wheatley and Jacobs embodied the practical-critical problems of interpretive resistance. And as their male counterparts do, they situate the intermediate texts in a sequence that moves from the compromised and hegemonized Wheatley (captured in the image of Wheatley's examination by white male elites) to the unexpectedly assertive voice of Jacobs (exemplified in the late critical discovery of her authorship). Much as we need not read a Moses Roper or Henry Bibb, thanks to Douglass, we can likewise extrapolate and bypass readings of Sojourner Truth or Jarena Lee by situating them in this trajectory.

Beyond Douglass: New Perspectives on Early African-American Literature takes as its starting point precisely this familiar disconnect between the teaching of, and the research about, early African-American letters. We do not mean to suggest that most or even many teachers of these writers and works have these views and perhaps could more accurately reframe what we have described as a disconnection between scholarship and

teaching as one between centripetal and centrifugal interpretive strategies, the former simplifying, streamlining, and encoding the tidy narratives of cultural development, the latter problematizing the same. Indeed,
far from being the site of simplification, the classroom may be the space
in which we are most acutely aware of these conflicting tendencies,
as the conventional survey form, the massive anthology, and especially
the comparative essay question together affirm and reinforce the very
national narratives we want to challenge. But if we have so far placed the
onus of simplification on classroom practices, opposed to an imaginary
field of nuanced research, we should now turn to the tacit streamlinings
that occur in the critical vocabulary of scholarship.

A useful exhibit here is the roundtable Historicizing Race in Early
American Studies, prepared by Sandra M. Gustafson for a recent issue
of *Early American Literature* and featuring position statements from
Joanna Brooks, Philip Gould, and David Kazanjian. Each participant
was presumably chosen for having written a recent monograph treating
"race,"[2] but all seem to have been selected as well for their divergent
methodological views. Indeed, it is tempting to imagine that the positions of this discussion were offered as an implicit narrative, in which
Brooks, with her emphasis on the *experience* of race, occupies a primal
position, followed by Gould's discursive problematization, and concluding with Kazanjian's attempts to split the difference.

Brooks takes as her starting point a definition of race as the effect of
organized social relations of domination—that is, race is first and fore-
most a matter of "how it is *experienced* by people of color" rather than
"imagined or intended by white people" (313, emphasis added). Any
legitimate study of race must thus be one that "repositions people of
color as the subjects of their own histories and intellectual traditions"
(315). If racial concepts were crafted by whites and then "imposed upon
people of color," that imposition was ultimately less a discursive transfer
than one dimension of an amalgam of brutal practices of exploitation
and domination (316). In the face of such harsh realities, people of color
reclaimed, redetermined, and renovated racial concepts, asserting ultimate ownership as those who experienced race (315, 316). There is no
doubt that this analytic insists that we keep our attention on the often
nontextualized realities of enslavement, colonization, resistance, and

community formation. It likewise has the virtue of insisting on a dialogue with contemporary ethnic studies scholarship and politics, as evidenced by Brooks's citation of more than three dozen twentieth-century academics, many of them theorists of race and ethnicity.

But one may also notice in this critical framework two suppositions that shape any application of these insights. Temporally, this experiential framework assumes that cultural reclamation and renovation *follow* earlier stages of experiential solidarity in the form of recognition of shared vulnerability and the initiation of collective action. As a result, the details of the difficult formation of this literary tradition may be somewhat muted. Spatially, it similarly follows that the collective social experience will trump the occasional individual aberration: in insisting that we "concentrate on the ways early Black and Native texts mattered to communities of color" (315), we are committed to a kind of feedback loop in which general orientations take precedence over particular articulations (315). The consequences of these assumptions perhaps become apparent when Brooks quotes Olaudah Equiano's narrative at the moment when he writes that not only was "slavery dreadful; but the state of a free negro appeared to me now equally so at least, and in some respects even worse" (317). Presented as a clear political position, the passage prompts a factual gloss, explaining other injustices experienced by Equiano and reminding us of "the enslavement of millions of Africans and the enslavement, death, and expropriation of millions of indigenous peoples in the Americas" (317). To highlight other elements of the passage—a fragmented sense of Black experience, for example, or possible contradictions with Equiano's Central American venture— would seem to border on an ethical breach.

It is in the space of such details that the next position, the discourse analysis here in the roundtable represented by Gould, joins the discussion. If Brooks had read the African-American tradition as a series of experience-based reclamations, Gould saw the critical construction of the tradition itself as a reclamation of a particular sort, often misreading earlier moments in its presentation of a unified story. That story, one in which eighteenth-century writings were but the stirrings of an African-American literary tradition that would reach fruition in the twentieth century, applied the "vocabularies of race and racism backwards" to find an aesthetic foundation and draw diachronic connections (322). Consequently contemporary critics, theoretically bound to notions of " 'ethnic' authenticity" (quote and scare quotes from Paul Gilroy), betrayed a commitment to strong misreadings that could be corrected only when they became attuned to critical "dissonance" (324, 322). Thus Gould's final statement on the matter: "I trust my archive more than their politics" (327). What exactly constitutes this broader and more complex archive? For one thing it would have to include white writers addressing race, an examination that would show how "language traded on the categories of race and culture" (323). In *Barbaric Traffic*, Gould had specifically explored the ways in which the discourses of race and slavery, on the one hand, and commerce and manners, on the other, were mutually "imbricated." The consequent instability or "elasticity" of terms, far from mitigating our sense of early American racism, reveals its broader constitutive presence. But at the same time it puts an almost fatal pressure on the notion of a "Black public sphere" separable from its white counterpart (324), and thus conceived as if language referred solely to experience and not to other language.

6

The contrast with Brooks's position is stark and is perhaps illustrated in the title of Gould's contribution, "What We Mean When We Say 'Race'," the scare quotes in this case calling as much attention to *Say* as to *Race* itself. In place of Brooks's experiential position, Gould stresses speech or print acts that differ in the degree to which they annunciate strong claims of contiguity linking commerce and slavery, race and manners. In the public sphere, these speech/print acts function as *memes*, each tangling with others as salient constellations of meaning, inclusive of both strategic elisions and ideological oversights, take form. If Gould's piece offers brief but nuanced discursive analyses of the kind that Brooks does not venture—for instance a reading of an 1808 sermon by the African-American minister Peter Williams (325)—it nonetheless takes the discursive field for granted as the only game in town and itself sidesteps the problem Michel-Rolph Trouillot calls "the moment of fact assembly (the making of *archives*)" (26). Thus if Gould offers interesting reflections on Phillis Wheatley's use of the phrase *sable race*, comparing it with later usage in *Frank Leslie's Illustrated Newspaper* (326), the critic's gravitation toward this expression, and the comparative archive it implies, is not a problem to be posed. Put more bluntly, the emphasis on the archive almost precludes discussions of the non- or less discursive practices of slavery that Brooks rightly emphasizes. If Gould may legitimately ask Brooks about the archive of her politics, she may in turn ask Gould about the politics of his archive.

In our view, neither of these positions may be dismissed, and we suspect that in the classroom both positions seem necessary and compelling. As we suggested earlier, the major pedagogical challenge may be the mediation of these two tendencies so convincingly enacted in scholarship. Kazanjian's attempt to find a position between two well-established theoretical positions begins with an endearing admission of uncertainty—he offers a critique of his own work, *The Colonizing Trick*, as a type of "obsessive recording of mastery"[3]—while explicitly treating the challenges faced in mediating experience and textuality. Kazanjian is clear in his hesitations toward Brooks's experiential approach, citing Miranda Joseph's critique of the "community" concept and Saidiya V. Hartman's analysis of the construction of the subjectivity of the enslaved (330). The skepticism toward Gould's discourse-analytical position is less clear, expressed as mystification at "a certain mechanistic and antiquarian conception of history," and an equally vague and rhetorical questioning of archival choices (331). More lucid, though, is his account of his own theoretical project, grounded on the "imbrications"—a term that recurs frequently in his essay—of "emergent, modern conceptions of race, nation, and equality" (331). Here Kazanjian is not far from Gould, who had similarly stressed the imbrication of racial concepts with those of commerce and trade. But where Gould had taken imbrication as a discursive quality of intersection, Kazanjian, whose project sought "to theorize the mode of that imbrication," argued that the connections between racial discourses and nationalism required a fundamental rethinking of both, for the combination of these discourses in a "racial nationalism" simultaneously created a "process of subjection" *and* "the very condition of possibility for the formal and abstract notion of equality" (332). In short, "equality was not restricted or contradicted by racial nationalism" but was rather "animated *by* and articulated *with* racial nationalism" (332). These two discourses were not contradictory, but rather complementary. This position then posed its own challenges to the experiential approach of Brooks, by insisting that experienced racial identities were paradoxically the effects of racial nationalism—effects the ramifications of which its created subjects often did not appreciate or perceive.

As for Gould's commitment to the archive, this was answered in Kazanjian's choice of texts "from social movements on the geographic borders of the early American empire" (333)—here a relatively unknown 1834 letter from one Samson Ceasar, an African-American émigré to Liberia in 1834. Ceasar seemed, at first glance, to reiterate certain racial stereotypes concerning unmotivated and unsuccessful immigrants from rural plantation slavery (334). But at another level, his account indirectly expressed the inseparability of slavery and freedom—"intimately and differentially related" (335). Tied to its Liberian situation, texts like Ceasar's revealed the "meanings—both explicit *and inchoate*"—of freedom for Black Americans (336, emphasis added). If we should not trust the seemingly straightforward statements of experience, we should be equally cautious about seemingly unified texts, for their gaps and juxtapositions provided keys to the structures of their own creation. If Kazanjian began with an emphasis on the imbrication of different discourses, he ended with a slightly different focus on "improvisation," the term capturing the interplay between experience and text without the naïve commitment to either (336). Thus he answered Gould's appeal to the archive by privileging an archive attuned to experiential disruptions: one would have to be as wary of ostensibly unified texts as of ostensibly unified experiences.

We can return to our earlier discussion of the African-American canon with a few tentative observations. Not only do the Brooks and Gould positions—one stressing the particularities of African-American experience, the other stressing intertextual connections and the processes of cultural construction—capture the two dominant critical positions of today's academy, but one can imagine most teachers committed to both of these positions in the classroom. The typical teacher might in fact attempt to strike a careful balance between, on the one hand, locating a Wheatley or an Equiano within an emerging and strong countertradition and, on the other, discursively linking them with a national (or transatlantic) narrative and the still problematic formulation of "race." In this light, Kazanjian's attempt to mediate these two positions, while harder to translate into a corresponding pedagogical practice, seems an attempt to escape these binary positions. Two concerns seem to guide his ventured resolution. On the one hand, he advocates a reading practice focused on symptomatic disruptions, which could perhaps suggest a reading of African-American authors as crucial bridging figures; a John Marrant might articulate a distinctive Black tradition *and* connections with the European-American canon but he would be significant above all as an interpretive key to the tensions in the canon at large. On the other hand, Kazanjian's dual interest in geographically remote *and* social movement texts (here the letter of Liberian colonization) suggests a very different classroom practice in which the more historically individuated material context becomes an integral component of analysis. What emerges, when we put these two emphases together, is something of a cultural mapping of specific mediations, attuned to the uneven contours and conduits of culture while abrogating the national framework within which this binary best functions.

9

It thus turns out that Kazanjian's third position, far from being a simple compromise between identity politics and discourse analysis, in fact calls on discourse analysis to aid in the clarification of African-American experience. We might even say that it evokes that seemingly musty tradition of "literary history" that in earlier incarnations focused on regions, schools, and movements. Here we might reflect on the uneven situation of American literary history, such that a number of reformulations of the overall canon still tend to overshadow the recuperative and relatively neglected histories of African-American letters. This unevenness is abundantly apparent if we juxtapose any number of literary-historical syntheses (Tompkins's *Sensational Designs*, Sundquist's *To Wake the Nations*, or the various and recent encyclopedic works like the multivolume *Cambridge History of American Literature*) with works like Blyden Jackson's *A History of Afro-American Literature* (volume 1, 1746–1895, published in 1989) and Dickson D. Bruce Jr.'s *The Origins of African American Literature, 1680–1865* (2001). While the latter do indeed offer strong readings of the African-American canon, comparatively situating works in relation to one another, it remains difficult to see either the impact of such histories on anthologization or signs of a familiarity, among generalists, with the issues at stake in defining the smaller canon. An older collection, Dorothy Porter's impressive but now neglected *Early Negro Writing* (1971, rep. 1995), illustrates what is at stake in its differentiated literary history: sections focused on "Mutual Aid and Fraternal Organizations, 1792–1833"; "Societies for Educational Improvement, 1808–1836"; "Significant Annual Conferences, 1831–1837"; "To Emigrate or Remain at Home? 1773–1833"; "Spokesmen in Behalf of their 'Colored Fellow Citizens,' 1787–1815"; "Saints and Sinners, 1786–1836"; and "Narratives, Poems and Essays, 1760–1835." The recent anthology of *North Carolina Slave Narratives*, edited by William L. Andrews and colleagues, is similarly illustrative in this respect. Noting that "no other southern state can match the contemporary impact or continuing import of black North Carolina's contribution to American literature during the slave era," the editors "hesitate to speculate" on why this is so (14). While the problem may seem hopelessly old-fashioned, a throwback to state-based literary histories, it nonetheless underscores a set of determinants (coded here as "North Carolina") yet to be examined. Teachers who have never read Moses Roper, Lunsford Lane, Moses Grandy, or Thomas H. Jones may rightly wonder how their sense of "the" African-American canon might be challenged. The lesson would seem to be that the African-American canon, a conceptual fiction like its Euro-American counterpart, emerged gradually and with important differentiations, engaging "white" and other texts in different ways at different moments in time. Failing to note such differentiations simply drives us back to streamlined, artificially constructed canons.

We want to conclude, then, with a brief discussion of Olaudah Equiano's *Interesting Narrative*, taking into account its canonization, pedagogical position, theoretical encoding, and potential for reopening the problem of literary history. How we teach Equiano's *Narrative* illuminates our assumptions about the African-American canon, given that the author seems, in various guises and at various points in the text, exemplary African, aspirant Afro-British, pietist Christian, Caribbean and North American entrepreneur, Central American capitalist, and African emissary. And there is the suggestion, made by Vincent Carretta, that Equiano may have been a native North American.[4] Absent a richer literary history to situate Equiano's tremendous mobility or his participation in various social movements (Huntingdonian Methodism, British and plebeian naval service, colonization projects, or Igbo traditions, either in Africa or in the Carolinas), the most innovative classroom strategies may assume the feel of utilitarian or strategic bad faith. An instructor might begin, for instance, with an identitarian gambit, allowing Equiano to speak for the Middle Passage, before playing the discursive trump card, suggesting Equiano's American nativity and focusing attention on the author's rhetorical skill and cultural literacy. While such a pedagogical strategy may elicit admirable critical reflections among students, the result may also be that the mediation of substantial theoretical and critical problems is yielded to students as a matter of opinion or inclination, and thus abandoned as unsolvable.

There is no escaping the conclusion that this pedagogical bind is tacitly underwritten by most anthologizers when they include only the early chapters of the *Interesting Narrative,* a surprisingly consistent preference whether Equiano is included in (a) general surveys of American and British literature (including more chronologically focused surveys of early American literatures), (b) anthologies of African-American literature, or (c) more specialized collections informed by Paul Gilroy's conceptualization of the "Black Atlantic" or Ira Berlin's "Atlantic Creole."[5] Thus the selections in Carla Mulford's *Early American Writings,* one aim of which was to highlight "the diversity of interests and peoples" (xvii), underscore Equiano's formative African experience and feature the first-person narration of his encounter with the slave ship and the horrific Middle Passage (chapters 1 and 2). Henry Louis Gates makes similar choices in *The Norton Anthology of African American Literature* (chapters 1 and 2, with brief excerpts from 3 and 4), but here, alongside an emphasis on the lineal roots of a literary efflorescence, there is also an effort to trace the development of the literary tropes and genres that later continue to animate African-American writing. Both collections thus declare a fealty to a multiculturalist agenda in noting distinctive markers of ethnically authentic difference. Equiano's place in both American and British surveys of eighteenth-century and romantic literature points even more broadly to the challenge of fixing Equiano's "true" identity to any single national or ethnic tradition. One might then expect collections that foreground the "Black Atlantic" to open a more complicated portrait, but, as Gesa Mackenthun notes in her brief survey of the literary anthologies that include *The Interesting Narrative*, its "anthologization . . . has largely followed suit in excluding the transoceanic element of Equiano's life."[6] Of all the anthologies, only Carretta's *Unchained Voices*, for instance, includes substantial passages from Equiano's travels postdating his manumission. When push comes to shove, and when space is limited, anthologizers generally opt for the conventionally teachable, but indisputably derivative, material from the beginning of the text, leaving teachers to decide whether and how to address the challenging questions raised by the now widely circulated if still relatively specialized knowledge concerning both Equiano's nativity and heavy reliance on Anthony Benezet's descriptions of Guinea.[7]

How, then, would one activate the rich potential of the *Interesting Narrative*? How could the narrative be something other than a text abridged and parsed for anthologies, and instead become a sort of anthology in itself? What, we wonder, would be the result of teaching more segments of the text—not just the African and Middle Passage chapters, but also, say, the chapters treating Central America and interactions with slaves and Indians, Equiano's religious conversion and proselytizing efforts, or his experiences in Savannah, Georgia. The purchase of such an approach would be more than a detailed familiarity with Equiano, rather opening up a number of traditions within Afro-Atlantic writing that, in turn, could illuminate and destabilize the Euro-American canon. Of course, one of the challenges of teaching Equiano are the idiosyncratic, if not exceptional, *experiences* he narrates. With students whose knowledge of slavery and the Atlantic slave trade is generally thin and circumscribed by depictions of U.S. antebellum plantation culture, there is a strong impulse to explain how Equiano's life was atypical, the vast majority of African slaves transferred to brutally regimented and dehumanizing labor camps in the West Indies. As long as we expect Equiano to channel the experiences of plantation slaves, or conversely sidestep that connection, then we are stuck between two monolithic positions: Equiano as generic eyewitness or Equiano as idiosyncratic speaker. An alternative approach would find in Equiano an encyclopedia of nodal points where discourse and experience meet. If

Equiano did not experience the Middle Passage, he surely emerged from a community in which that experience was richly articulated. Nevertheless, this one node is not exhaustive. No one of Equiano's disparate experiences ought to sustain alone a singular or even representative identity; rather, his travels and affiliations should serve as resonant material conditions from which his multiple personae emerge, and they structure how these identities were made legible, were disseminated, and ultimately were received.

If Equiano's *Interesting Narrative* has the potential to highlight the multiple originary points of African-American literatures, it could also invite us to rethink the tradition of the fugitive slave narrative itself. If critics have been challenging the hegemony of that tradition in recent years, this has been as much a reaction against its critical streamlining (as per the Olney framework mentioned earlier) as a commentary on any actual generic continuities. Indeed, the impetus for this collection was our own pedagogical experiences substituting or adding different slave narratives in American literature surveys. Teaching William Grimes's 1825 *Life*, a fascinatingly litigious narrative ranging from Virginia to New Haven, and relatively untouched by the abolition movement, gave to students a very different sense of African-American literary interventions than the more familiar Douglass story. The same was true with the enormous "Charles Ball" narrative, *Slavery in the United States* (1836), a massive ethnographic narrative chronicling the migration of the peculiar institution to Georgia; or the Lewis and Milton Clarke narratives (1846), with their elaborate satirical appendixes and a very different Kentuckian orientation to abolition; or Henry Bibb's 1849 narrative of flight, return, flight, and return, centered on his relationship with his wife; or the amazing narrative of Sojourner Truth, with its details about New York slavery and religious innovations; or Solomon Northup's *Twelve Years a Slave* (1853), which recounts his life as a free man in New York before being kidnapped and sold into slavery in Louisiana.[8] One could mention as well the narratives of Moses Roper, William Wells Brown, Josiah Henson, William and Ellen Craft, or Jacob Green. Any one of these texts, in the classroom, reorients the very presentation of "American literature," becoming much more than a minor variant of Douglass. And venturing away from Douglass, about whom a surprising

13

percentage of students have already learned the canonical interpretation, usefully disrupts the notion of the representative writer.

A more charitably descriptive approach to slave narratives also suggests ways to be less prescriptive about which texts belong in the representation of the African-American literary tradition. Later, Xiomara Santamarina describes a cohort of African-American texts whose orientation is not determined by the movement politics of abolitionism. A more generous approach invites these narrative experiments back in from the margins, makes space for them in the various traditions of the early African-American canon. As we are encouraged to explore the fascinating travels of Nancy Prince to czarist Russia in the mid-nineteenth century, we may also make space for other literary experiments outside the U.S. experience as well into the antebellum and postwar periods and yet still within the field of study designated nominally as African-American writing. Notable here is the republication of Maxwell Philip's *Emmanuel Appadocca, or The Blighted Life* (University of Massachusetts Press, 1997) and the anonymous *Adolphus, A Tale* (University of the West Indies Press, 2003), two novels written in the 1850s in Trinidad that, while self-consciously responsive to the passage of the Fugitive Slave Law in the United States, also explore caste-stratified social and cultural identities in the post-emancipation Caribbean. As William E. Cain writes in his introduction to *Emmanuel Appadocca*, connecting that novel not only to *Uncle Tom's Cabin* and *Moby-Dick*, its contemporaries, but to Richard Wright's *Native Son* (1940), Ralph Ellison's *Invisible Man* (1952), and James Baldwin's *Go Tell It on the Mountain* (1953), and plays such as Langston Hughes's *Mulatto* (1935) and Imamu Amiri Baraka's *Dutchman* (1964), *The Slave* (1964), and *Slave Ship* (1967), "it is, again, a different kind of book, one that both does and does not derive and develop its meanings from slavery and abolition" (lv, xxxvii).

In compiling *Beyond Douglass: New Perspectives on Early African-American Literature*, we sought essays reflecting upon the developing canon, considering more thoughtful course design, perhaps even suggesting anthology reform. In the spirit of practical innovations, we invited our contributors to use this forum to draw on specialized scholarly expertise to address fellow teachers of American literature. The first three chapters of *Beyond Douglass* work at the intersections of religious expression

and communal identity. Katherine Faull presents the interpretive difficulties scholars face when they enter the archive of early African-
American writing. Her exploration of two Moravian funeral memoirs,
each written by a former Black slave, attends to questions of genre,
mode, polyvocality, and reception. Faull shows us that African-
American autographs are most fruitfully explored as *practices.* The autograph is neither the passive receptor and conduit of norms for subjective
expression, nor wholly empowered to speak in her own voice. Instead,
the "speaking subject plays with signifying, by means of the rhetorical
strategies of displacement and metalepsis, but that same subject is also
. . . played with. The Black autograph extends and subverts the dominant discourses of European culture, but . . . these discourses still define
the process of self-differentiation" (27). We are grateful not only to be
able to present Faull's work to a new audience—her essay first appeared
in a publication directed at Germanists—but to print for the first time
together and complete Faull's transcriptions and translations of the
memoirs themselves. Handwritten in German and stored in the   15
Moravian Archives in Bethlehem, Pennsylvania, the memoirs of
Andrew and Magdalene are now available for broader scholarly and
pedagogical use.[9]

April Langley extends Faull's account of rhetorical practices to
show how biblical literacy empowered Black authors actively to partici-
pate in exegesis and hermeneutics. Phillip M. Richards connects
African-American writing to the task of social formation, a link between
writing and materiality that unearths surprising parallels between the
communal strategies employed by white Protestant pietists and their
dissenters and African-American clerics and later secular Black reformers. Commenting on the Black elites' cultivation of charismatic legitimacy and their appropriation of the voices of the "wretched" Black
masses, Richards explains that early writers sought a "political fulfillment grounded primarily in institutional achievement" (85). This char-
acterization runs against the tendency of reading Black writing as
making more generally universalistic or humanist claims. Barriers to full
civic participation and communal integrity ultimately led Black authors
toward "proto-romantic interpretations of their contemporary African
American condition" (89). Richards suggests the thematic comparison

of nineteenth-century Black writing to the romantic alienation expressed in the work of Emerson and the young Karl Marx. "The black minister-writers initiated a tradition in which African-American intellectuals recognize a similar objectification in their own experience, an alienating process stemming from a dehumanizing estrangement from civic and social life" (90).

The next group of chapters make for an interesting pair. They consider African-American, or, to cite Ira Berlin, Atlantic Creole writing, within multiple discursive, cultural, and material circuits of exchange. Vincent Carretta and Philip Gould clearly have affinities. Both reject the narrowness of a literary canon defined by national belonging, preferring the more capacious category of the trans- or circum-atlantic. Both suspect the ascription of value to early Black writing with reference to a later canon formation whether based on ethno-traditional, aesthetic, or national foundations. But Carretta's insistence on "language, period, phenotype" retains an identitarian prescription that Gould's references to William Cowper, Henry David Thoreau, and William Lloyd Garrison mitigate. This difference is perhaps exaggerated here to highlight more subtle distinctions. Both Carretta and Gould feature, in Carretta's words, "primacy of chronology," that is, treating Black writing with reference to the historicity of production and reception. To be fair, it is not as if Gould displaces the importance of phenotype completely. But rather than see Blackness solely or primarily as a constituent of experience, he is interested in how Black *writing* intervenes in a broader discursive field. The difference may boil down to Carretta's privileging of the writing subject and Gould's insistence on the intertextual subject matter. Gould indeed does note one of the dangers of the discursive field: "Sentimentalizing the horrors of slavery often led to the narrative erasure of Africans themselves, usually in violent death or even tragic suicide" (128). But he turns this around by pointing out that the writers were themselves aware of and sensitive to "the terms in which these debates were waged" (130). If rhetorical positioning can be said to jeopardize the vitality of Black experience, the rich rhetorical skills of Black writers are in part recuperative, restoring a type of subjective agency through "rhetorical management." If Carretta positions Black writers as

16

expressive of "overlapping, rather than conflicting, identities" (112), Gould imagines them as their own ideal audience, as skillful at *reading* as at writing the conditions of their participation in the public sphere.

John Saillant also stresses the broadly discursive literacy of Black writers but places the emphasis on a civic literacy that he sees absent in our own historical moment. Indeed, Saillant argues that reencountering African-Americans' aspirant citizenship would be a way to educate our students about the values of democratic participation and republican values. In our own cynical age—with our preferences for irony over sincerity—we may miss how Black writers were "expressing their sense of citizenship—not ironically but insistently and prospectively" (148). African-American writers, Saillant argues, "had a clearer understanding of the founding of the new nation than many in our time who have not only the opportunity but also the responsibility to know better" (142). Saillant urges us to take seriously the sincerity with which African-American writers pursued civic participation, evident in the appropriation of its public vocabulary, or grammar. African-American writers drew on their appreciation for and understanding of republican ideals when they pursued civic engagement through the normative device of the petition form, for example, using phrases, concepts, and cadences of widely read republican texts like Thomas Paine's *American Crisis, The Federalist*, and the U.S. Constitution.

The last two essays suggest ways to broaden what we teach when we represent African-American writing to our students. As alluded to previously, Xiomara Santamarina extends the discursive literacy of antebellum Black writing by pointing out the wider scope of interests manifest in midnineteenth-century African-American writing. Santamarina's chapter surveys a fascinating set of largely unexplored writings that continue to put pressure on any unified notion of an African-American literary canon. One outshoot is that Douglass's "exemplary" slave narrative appears the result of a finely tuned and highly crafted mode of life writing carefully fitted to the exigencies of white abolitionism. If less stylistically coherent, other Black slave autographs achieve greater autonomy outside the dictates of movement politics. And Black writers quickly learned to satisfy the supplementary use-value of slave narratives to white audiences, that is, for entertainment. Black writers also explored the challenges of realizing the benefits of freedom in the nonslaveholding North, the assumption of privilege by aspirant middle-class free Blacks, and the formation of elite worldliness among those African-Americans who described their travels abroad. Especially noteworthy are the *Life and Travels* of Nancy Prince, who wrote of her travel to czarist Russia and her subsequent missions to Jamaica and work on behalf of emancipated Jamaican slaves. As Santamarina writes, Prince's writing testifies to the "challenges that regional or class-based *intraracial* difference posed (and still poses) to our assumptions of diasporic transnational racial solidarity, or "imagined communities" (172). "The point," she writes, "is to complicate students' understandings of what constitute raced texts and Black authors' audiences so that they can better appreciate the multiple or heterogeneous traditions African American writers inaugurated and revised (178).

If Santamarina compels us to see a broad diversity among disparate African-American writers, Robert S. Levine challenges us to recognize the changeable and even contradictory views held by those individual authors who have assumed canonical status through the celebration of exemplary and frequently singular works of genius. By asking us to privilege the study of the career over the study of the monument, Levine further contextualizes acts of political and aesthetic engagement. Would Douglass be baffled by our pedagogical obsession with his 1845 narrative, written at the very beginning of a career that would last another fifty years? What would William Wells Brown think of our fixation on *Clotel*, "though there is absolutely no indication in any of Brown's writing that he regarded the 1853 *Clotel* as having a special status in his career" (182)? Levine's insights result from his editing of the works of Brown and Delany, which has given him a wariness about narrowly univocal biographical or formalist readings. Nonplussed by the apparent contradictions a study of careers reveals, Levine prefers these to the static approach to monumental works because "such a perspective . . . allows for a greater interpretive freedom to engage texts as part of an ongoing cultural conversation" (197), one that ultimately extends to us and our students.

Notes

1. See James Olney, "Master Plan for Slave Narratives," (50–51) in James Olney, " 'I Was Born a Slave': Slave Narratives, Their Status as Autobiography and as Literature," *Calla* 100 no. 20 (Winter, 1934): 46–73.

2. Brooks published *American Lazarus: Religion and the Rise of African-American and Native American Religions* in 2003 and had coedited, with John Saillant, the aforementioned anthology *'Face Zion Forward.'* Gould published *Barbaric Traffic: Commerce and Antislavery in the Eighteenth-Century Atlantic World* in 2003 and coedited, with Vincent Carretta, *Genius in Bondage: Literature of the Early Black Atlantic* in 2001; Kazanjian published *The Colonizing Trick: National Culture and Imperial Citizenship in Early America* in 2003 and coedited *Loss: The Politics of Mourning* with David Eng in 2002.

3. See 332–33 and 336; the citation is from an unpublished paper by Fred Moten.

4. Vincent Carretta, "Olaudah Equiano or Gustavus Vassa? New Light on an Eighteenth-Century Question of Identity," *Slavery and Abolition* 20 (1999): 96–105.

5. The provenance of these labels is discussed in Carretta's essay in this volume. Referenced anthologies include Nina Baym, ed., *The Norton Anthology of American Literature*, 6th ed. (New York: W. W. Norton, 2003); Paul Lauter, ed., *The Heath Anthology of American Literature*, 5th Ed. (Boston: Houghton Mifflin, 2006); David Damrosch and Kevin J. H. Dettmar, eds., *The Longman Anthology of British Literature*, 3rd ed. (New York: Pearson Longman, 2006); Carla Mulford, ed., *Early American Writing* (New York: Oxford University Press, 2002); Susan Castillo and Ivy Schweitzer, eds., *The Literatures of Colonial America* (Malden, MA: Blackwell, 2001); Myra Jehlen and Michael Warner, eds., *The English Literatures of America* (New York: Routledge, 1997); Henry Louis Gates, ed., *The Norton Anthology of African American Literature*, 2nd ed. (New York: W. W. Norton, 2004); Adam Potkay and Sandra Burr, eds., *Black Atlantic Writers of the 18th Century: Living the Exodus in England and the Americas* (New York: St Martin's Press, 1995). and Vincent Carretta, ed., *Unchained Voices: Anthology of Black Authors in the English-Speaking World of the 18th Century* (Lexington: University of Kentucky Press, 1996).

6. Gesa Mackenthun, *Fictions of the Black Atlantic in American Foundational Literature* (London: Routledge, 2004) 38.

7. To their credit, the editors of *The Heath Anthology of American Literature*, the *Longman Anthology of British Literature*, and *The Norton Anthology of African American Literature* explain to students that Equiano may have been born in South Carolina and thus not have experienced himself the events narrated in chapters 1 through 4. Neither Mulford nor the editors of *The Norton Anthology of British Literature* do so.

8. The Grimes, Ball, Clarke, Bibb, and Northup narratives are all available in Yuval Taylor's excellent two-volume anthology *I Was Born a Slave*; the Sojourner Truth narrative, first published in 1850 but revised and expanded in 1884, appears in an excellent Penguin edition edited by Nell Irvin Painter.

9. Of note is that Magdalene's owner, Charles Brockden, was the great uncle of the early American writer Charles Brockden Brown.

Self-Encounters: Two Eighteenth-Century Memoirs from Moravian Bethlehem

In almost all colonial situations, the fight for liberty begins at the point where the colonized appears to be integrated into the culture of the colonizer; at the point where the colonized appears to be linguistically and therefore culturally linked with the colonizer.

—S. E. Ogude, *Genius in Bondage*

Introduction

DEEP IN THE VAULT OF THE MORAVIAN ARCHIVES IN BETHLEHEM, Pennsylvania, lie two African autobiographies written in German from the middle of the eighteenth century.[1] The authors are husband and wife, Andrew and Magdalene, who use their Christian names—and I use that term advisedly. Andrew, an Igbo, went to Moravian Bethlehem in 1746 at the age of sixteen. Magdalene, from Little Popo on the Gold Coast, had arrived in Bethlehem three years earlier when she was twelve. These African teenagers were two of the earliest inhabitants of Moravian Bethlehem, a settlement that had been founded only in 1741. The Moravian Church, or Brüdergemeinde, as it is known in Germany, claims its pre-Reformation origins in what is today the Czech Republic. After three centuries of persecution in Moravia, Bohemia, and Poland, the Moravian Church was "renewed" in the early eighteenth century by the pietist Count Ludwig von Zinzendorf. In 1722 Zinzendorf extended an invitation to the persecuted Moravians to settle on his estate in Upper Saxony. To this small number of "refugees" were soon added scores of artisans, peasants, and craftsmen who went to the Moravian Church in search of freedom to develop their individual spirituality and practice communal faith. The Moravian movement spread to North America in 1740.

Andrew and Magdalene married in 1762 and had three children, two boys and a girl, who all died in infancy. Andrew died in 1779 at the age of fifty. Magdalene lived for almost another forty years, dying in her eighty-ninth year. This whole African Moravian family, children and parents, are buried in the God's Acre cemetery in Bethlehem. Only three graves are to be found today. Andrew's lies on the northernmost side of the graveyard with those of the other married men. Magdalene's lies in the center among the married women, and their one baptized child, also named Andrew, lies among the children. Their position in death reflects their place in life as members of the Moravian congregation in Bethlehem. Identified primarily through their allegiance with a "choir," that is, a spiritual grouping based on marital status, gender, and age and not on familial ties, these graves lie alongside those of German artisans and nobility, next to Delawares and Wampanos, next to European settlers of colonial America. In a strangely parallel fashion the memoirs of Andrew and Magdalene lie in boxes on the archive shelves, slipped between the life stories of other non-African Moravians. Until recently the existence of these two documents was unrecorded by anyone outside the Moravian Archives.[2] And until now, they have not been discussed at all either in the exploration of cultural connections between Germany and Africa or in examinations of the interconnectedness of race, gender, and the autobiographical act.

Moravian authors usually begin their memoirs by citing their birthplace and parentage—invariably somewhere in Europe or colonial America. For example, Anna Boehler writes, "I was born on January 1, 1740, in Germantown in the county of Philadelphia in the state of Pennsylvania. My late father was Peter Rose, a native of Bohemia, who left Moravia for his freedom of conscience and to ensure his salvation, as did also my dear mother Catharina Huber, and both came to Herrnhut."[3] Or Paul Münster writes, "I was born in 1716 on July 25 in Zauchenthal in Moravia. My parents were in the Ancient Brethren's Church, led a godfearing life and used diligently the books of the Ancient Brethren. We children were encouraged in learning and reading and were prevented through discipline and order from keeping any kind of bad company."[4] Imagine my surprise when I find a Moravian memoir that begins, "I, Andrew the Moor, was born in Iboland, in the unknown part of Africa and according to the customs of my nation was circumcised when I was 8 days old. My name was Ofodobendo Wooma."[5] Or, less exotically and more poignantly, the beginning of Magdalene's memoir, "I was, as is known, a slave or the property of the late Mr. Brockden, who bought me from another master when I was ten years old, and from then on I served his family until I was grown up."[6]

On reading these unconventional opening sentences, my first reaction is to ask, How should these memoirs be interpreted? Can they be analyzed with the same tools as memoirs by European and European-American authors? Certainly, Andrew's and Magdalene's memoirs are determined to a degree by the expectations of every Moravian about their spirituality and the relation of that spiritual life to other Moravians. However, Andrew and Magdalene were narrating their spiritual lives to an audience with specific notions about the possibility of Africans possessing "souls" and what the path could be toward finding that soul. This audience was the Moravian community in Bethlehem, Pennsylvania. I wish to explore in this essay how the expectations of that audience shaped these memoirs, that is, how the Moravian notions of identity, race, and gender provided frameworks within which Andrew and Magdalene encountered their autobiographical selves. For example, what discursive modes existed in Moravian writing—writing that was definitely part of the Western Enlightenment "discovery" of the self—that could act as idioms for African self-writing? How did these African authors embellish or deviate from the form of the Moravian spiritual memoir in what Ogude in the epigraph to this essay terms "the fight for liberty"?[7]

23

Gender, Race, and the Spiritual Autobiography

In the Western tradition, the autobiographical genre has been understood as both an encounter with and a relation of selfhood. It stresses the unique nature of an individual's life as lived, remembered, and related. What is told about a life can be a complex fabric of projection, desire, and experience, all of which join to represent a subjectivity encountered through the text. Traditionally, much scholarship on the history and theory of autobiography has assumed the writing subject to be male and white, and this assumption has had a significant effect on the conceptualization of the autobiographical act. Critics have claimed that the autograph is one who recognizes himself as a unique being, not to be repeated in time, and that the autobiographical act is one of drawing together the disparate pieces of life through a single unifying consciousness.[8] The only relationship the white male autograph needs is with himself as both the subject and the object of the writing.

In sharp contrast to such a model of life writing, women's studies scholars such as Mary Mason, Patricia Spacks, Estelle Jelinek, and Carolyn Heilbrun have turned to the eighteenth century to examine the earliest form of women's writing—the spiritual confessional.[9] These scholars have argued that the paradigm for women's life writing is the spiritual autobiography in which the woman defines herself in relation to an other, Christ. The writing subject, it has been argued, does not consider herself to be an autonomous and unique being whose life story is being shaped by the unifying story of the autobiography. Rather, the female autograph depicts a radically different notion of subjectivity in the relation of her life: her self-relation fundamentally questions the Enlightenment notion of the autonomous self/subject in that she constitutes her life story in an intersubjective "conversation" with an other or others (in the case of the spiritual narrative, with Christ; or, in a communal society, with others within that communal structure). It has been argued that the grounding of female self-identity in the consciousness of another, usually Christ, has enabled the women to "write openly about themselves."[10] In what appears to be almost a dialogue with Jesus the female subject finds her voice. The problem with such a concept of identity is that this "relational female self" with "permeable ego boundaries" can lead to "a kind of selfless abnegation."[11]

The expectations of the audience in the social and economic environment of the eighteenth-century slave trade also determined the voice or voices in which the African and black autograph was able to tell his or her life. The autograph could not assume the individual identity of the white male or female and be believed but, rather, had to portray him- or herself as a token of a type. The black and/or female autograph told narratives that appealed to what Robert B. Stepto has termed "white America's credulity."[12] In his study of the nineteenth-century slave narrative, Stepto delineates the ways in which the black author would win that credulity, ways that shaped black narrative through, for example, the increasing incorporation of authenticating materials into his or her story. In order to gain the ear of white America, the black narrator, both male and female, had to assume a voice that would be believed. In the earlier forms of black writing, authenticating documents were appended to the author's text (see, for example, the list of Boston dignitaries that gives witness to the "authenticity" of Wheatley's poetry),[13] whereas the later nineteenth-century narratives totally subsumed authenticating strategies into the personal account.[14] When appealing to a white audience, Stepto and others have argued, black narratives have always had to combine, integrate, and conflate the personal and individual story of the author with an authenticating "white realism," which was recognizable and credible to a white audience.

Two hundred years ago, in an era in which the possibility of the existence of an African soul was questioned by Western thinkers and politicians, autobiography was, to a great extent, the instrument with which the selfhood of the African, whether slave or free, could be expressed. Often, however, it was determined both positively and negatively by the "white man's idiom."[15]

And what was that idiom? The dominant discourses of self in the late eighteenth century, discourses that would be credible to a non-African audience in both Europe and colonial America, were those of the religious conversion narrative, the travel narrative, and later the slave narrative. Certainly, deployment of these narrative forms varied from autograph to autograph. For example, the spiritual narrative provided an appropriate idiom for John Marrant's *A Narrative of the Lord's Dealings with John Marrant* (1785).[16] The antislave polemic shaped Ottobah Cuguano's *Thoughts and Sentiments on the Evil of Slavery* (1787).[17] The spiritual, abolitionist, polemic, and Robinsonade narrative informed that more famous eighteenth-century Igbo text, Olaudah Equiano's *The Interesting Narrative of the Life of Olaudah Equiano or the African, written by Himself* (1789).[18] Over the last ten to fifteen years reception of these texts has moved from considering them as reliable historical accounts to regarding them rather as palimpsests, multivocal relations of lives marked by displacement, alienation, and the experience of prejudice. And, as Henry Louis Gates Jr. has pointed out, this interpretive shift has also radically affected the understanding of blackness as existing in a unified knowable Black self. As Gates points out, identification of multiple narrative voices challenges "the single most pervasive and consistent assumption of all black writing since the eighteenth century . . . [namely,] that there exists an unassailable, integral, black self, as compelling and as whole in Africa as in the New World, within slavery as without slavery. What's more, this self was knowable, retrievable, recuperable, if only enough attention to detail were displayed."[19]

26

If we take Equiano's text as an example of this shift in interpretation, we can identify in the last decade the move from those who have attempted to locate Equiano's home in Igboland[20] (to the great pleasure of Isseke's present-day inhabitants) to those who have read his text as a gleaning of others' experiences that has been rewoven by the author in an attempt to place himself in eighteenth-century London society.[21] Even one of the most historicist readers of this narrative, Elizabeth Isichei, who, in her several books on the history of the Igbo people has used Equiano's narrative as a primary source, recently changed her mind about the historical reliability of Equiano's text. She now agrees that Equiano's Igbo past is mostly a reconstruction of European or colonial American travel narratives, most obviously, Anthony Benezet's *Some Historical Account of Guinea* (1771).[22]

So what sort of notion of self does this palimpsest of narrative voices reflect? Is it an unretrievable, fragmented Black identity, overdetermined by the dominant Western discourses of the eighteenth century? Or does the Black author use these voices to construct and thus encounter a coherent and differentiated self? The simultaneous presence in Olaudah Equiano's autobiography of at least three different voices has suggested a Bakhtinian reading of the polyphonic narrative of self to recent critics of the African-American and African eighteenth-century autobiography.[23] And through such a reading the polyphony of Black autobiography can be understood as a conscious and playful transgression of cultural, generic, and racial boundaries[24] as well as a semiconscious reflection of cross-cultural transmission of oral tropes.[25] However it is understood, the polyphony of eighteenth-century Black narrative is a constitutive act—one by which the self may be encountered as a speaking subject. This speaking subject plays with signifying, by means of the rhetorical strategies of displacement and metalepsis, but that same subject is also, as Gates and Bakhtin suggest, played with.[26] The Black autograph extends and subverts the dominant discourses of European culture, but, as I shall show, these discourses still define the process of self-differentiation, of identity—an identity in flux.

27

Moravian Memoirs

In order to read polyphony an audience has to know which voices are present, which stories are being told, and which story lines are being played with by the narrator. It is easier to examine such polyphony in Andrew's and Magdalene's memoirs in that there are so many with which an audience may compare them. In the same way as their memoirs would have been heard by an audience that had heard many others and thus were able to compare the narration of their lives with the narration of others' lives, so too in the late twentieth century I am able to read Andrew's and Magdalene's memoirs in the context of hundreds of others.[27] Reading through box after box of memoirs in the Moravian Archives, I can recognize a rhythm of autobiographical voice that varies somewhat from author to author but whose pattern of self-encounter remains steady. The Moravian memoir, designed to be read as a farewell gesture at the individual's funeral, should depict the spiritual growth of the individual. To this end, the memoirs frequently describe the innocence of childhood, a spiritually troubled adolescence, acquaintance with the Moravian Brethren, the journey to Bethlehem, reception into the congregation, first communion, employment, and maybe marriage. The memoir was frequently composed in old age and consisted of a retrospective appraisal of the individual's life. Its narrative structure and language reflect the author's consciousness that the memoir will be read aloud to the congregation only after the author has "gone home." On occasion, the memoir was written at a major turning point in life, before the individual's reception into the congregation or, in the case of women, before marriage.

From 1747 until the present day, each member of the Moravian community has been expected to write an account of his or her life to be read at the individual's funeral. The leader of the Moravians, Count Nikolaus Ludwig von Zinzendorf, introduced this custom for two reasons. First, he felt that the deceased should have a chance to say goodbye to the rest of the community, just as the members who heard these words would also be able to say their farewells. Second, Zinzendorf saw these documents as an important part of the history of the Moravian Church. As each individual maintained a different relationship with the Savior, every narrative added another unique piece to the overall picture of the community. Zinzendorf considered religion to be ecumenical: that is, it centers around a "tropos" or individual representation of Christ's life and death. Through this process, which in the Moravian memoir exists in the form of a dialogue with Christ, the individual is made highly conscious of Christ's presence in his or her life, making of the *Heiland* or Savior almost a tangible partner. Zinzendorf stressed the *personal* value of Christ's passion and death, what he terms the *ita sentio* (it seemed to me as though) of religious consciousness. A consciousness of Christ is made present through the power of the imagination, through the words of the text and the particularly active role of the creator of that text. Thus, every time a member of the Church wrote about her or his relationship to Christ it constituted a new and fresh trope of him.

Andrew and Magdalene were also expected to follow the pattern in their process of self-narration. However, what "white realisms" about Africa and Africans or non-African Moravians were in the minds of the congregation as they listened to Andrew's and Magdalene's memoirs? What kind of spiritual life was considered possible for them as "ex-heathens"?

First, the fact that they were both slaves was well known to their audience. Andrew and Magdalene had both been sold by their previous owners, Thomas Noble and Charles Brockden, respectively, to the trustees of Moravian Bethlehem (at that time Peter Boehler and August Spangenberg).[28] Magdalene begins her memoir, "I was, as is known, a slave or the property of the late Mr. Brockden," the Deputy Master of the Rolls of the Province of Pennsylvania and Recorder of Deeds, bought to be a maidservant to his wife. After her death she was sent to Bethlehem. Andrew's owners would also have been known to the audience. Thomas and Mary Noble were a wealthy merchant couple in New York City and had been supporters of the Moravian Church from its beginnings in the city. When Count Nikolaus Ludwig von Zinzendorf visited America in 1741, he stayed with them (Noble owned Andrew at that time and it is probable that they met). The Moravian congregation in New York met in Noble's house between 1741 and 1745, again the period during which Andrew was living there. Noble's maidservant, Eleanor Gregg, who became an ardent Moravian, in fact left New York City, went to Bethlehem, and married Hector Gambold, and as a couple they then returned to New York to work with the Moravians there. Andrew was thus a member of a wealthy and influential Moravian household. When Noble's wife died in 1745 Andrew was allowed to go to the congregation in Bethlehem along with Noble's children, Thomas, Isaac, James, Sarah, and Mary.

29

Also known to the audience were of course the history of the Moravian Church and its historical link with the missionary movement. The Moravian Church was an ancient Protestant church that had been founded in the fifteenth century by the followers of Jan Hus and had been revitalized in the early eighteenth century by the German nobleman Count Nikolaus Ludwig von Zinzendorf. Since this renewal, the Moravian Church had become increasingly active in the Protestant evangelical awakening in Germany, Great Britain, and North America, and in mission work. After the "mother" settlement, Herrnhut, had been successfully founded as a religious community, other centers were started in the Wetterau (now in Hessen in western Germany), Holland, Greenland, South Africa, Great Britain, Ireland, and the Caribbean. In 1740, after a failed attempt to start a community in Georgia, the

Moravians arrived at the forks of the Delaware River in Pennsylvania to found a religious community and, for the next eighty-five years, this community, Bethlehem was open only to members of the Moravian Church. Furthermore, for the first twenty-one years, it was run on purely communal principles. During this period, known as the "General Economy," there was no private property; all land, houses, and factories were communally owned. Women and men, even when married, were strictly segregated, living in common buildings or "choirs," and children were removed from their parents as soon as they were weaned and were placed in the "Nurserie." The communal principles of the "General Economy" were abandoned in 1763 purportedly because of an economic crisis in the Moravian Church in Germany. At that point, private property was permitted, families lived together, and the choir houses remained only for the unmarried and widowed men and women.

Bethlehem was founded as a mission center or *Pilgergemeinde:* that is, a community of individuals for whom missionary and spiritual work were of primary importance. Its purpose was to promulgate Christianity within North America and to act as a base for missionaries to the native North Americans and the slave plantations in the Caribbean. Within the structure of choirs, the individual brothers and sisters were able to devote their energies to the goal of the community: the formation of a steady religious and economic base, from which satellite mission communities (both in North America and abroad) could be supported.

The choir system also existed for theological reasons. Count Zinzendorf prescribed strict sexual segregation for the unmarried Moravians, both to help protect them from sexual desire and to promote spiritual life. Zinzendorf felt that spirituality was best developed in the individual by the ability to live and worship with persons of like age, gender, and marital status. In Bethlehem, there existed separate choirs for married persons, widows, widowers, unmarried men, unmarried women, adolescent men, adolescent women, boys, girls, and weaned toddlers. When Andrew and Magdalene joined the Moravians in Bethlehem they also lived with the choirs appropriate to their age, sex, and marital status. Andrew joined the Single Brethrens Choir and Magdalene the Single Sisters Choir. There they lived with Europeans, colonial and Native Americans, and other people of African origin.

Their lives in the choir houses were not distinguished by their race but rather by their social class; their spiritual growth was discussed with the Laborers of each choir. For Andrew, his "speakings," as they were called, took place initially with Brother Nathaniel Seidel, later leader of the Bethlehem congregation, and Magdalene's discussions of her troubled spiritual state were carried on with the laboress of the Single Sisters Choir, Anna Anders. Thus, Andrew's and Magdalene's lives within the Moravian community were recognizable. But what of their lives prior to joining the congregation? In what spiritual condition were they expected to have entered the Moravian Church?

In order to answer that question we have to look at the history of Moravianism within the eighteenth-century mission movement. The Moravians were not just an isolated Protestant group in Pennsylvania, but rather part of the most successful worldwide Protestant missionary organization in the eighteenth century. A central component of the Moravian Church from its renewal was its understanding of and commitment to work in the mission field. Necessarily, such work put the members of the church in close contact with cultures that were radically different from their own. From almost the outset of his involvement with Pietism and the Moravian Brethren, Zinzendorf was especially interested in the work of missions and the conversion of the "heathen." He had contact with mission work through the reports of two missionaries whom the Halle Pietist educator Augustus Hermann Francke had sent to Tranquebar.[29] Then, in 1732, even before he sent his own missionaries out into the field, Zinzendorf outlined his mission theology in a letter sent to Johann Ernst Geister, a missionary sent to Madras by the Stollberg *Konsistorium.* In this letter, he advises Geister of the appropriate demeanor toward the non-Christian. Zinzendorf writes: "Show a happy and lively spirit and in external matters do not rule over the heathen in the slightest fashion, but rather gain respect among them through the strength of your spirit, and in external matters humble yourself below them as much as possible."[30]

Zinzendorf was well aware of the problems missionaries had already encountered in their contacts with other cultures, problems he attributed to the attitude missionaries had adopted toward the non-Christian. For example, Zinzendorf claimed that the refusal of some missionaries to mix with the non-Christians, or to live at their level of poverty, was contrary to the spirit of Christ. Missionaries and non-Christians should both show deference only to the invisible Savior rather than the non-Christians showing deference to the Moravians.

Where did Zinzendorf get these ideas for such an egalitarian attitude toward the non-Christian, an attitude that caused the later Moravian missionaries in their mission on St. Thomas such great difficulties with the authorities?[31] It could be said that both the impetus to begin the first Moravian mission on St. Thomas and the stance to be adopted toward the slaves there came from the same source. In 1731, while on a visit to the court in Copenhagen, Count Zinzendorf met Anton, the slave of the director of the West Indian-Guinea Company, Count von Danneskjold-Laurvig. During this visit, Anton apparently recounted to Zinzendorf the story of his enslaved sister, who was still living on St. Thomas. He expressed the hope that if his sister were to hear the Gospel, as she desired, she and many other slaves there would convert to Christianity.[32]

Listening to Anton's words, Zinzendorf saw how his own desire to start a mission might be realized. In July 1731, Anton returned to Herrnhut with Zinzendorf, presented his story to the assembled Moravian Brethren there, and suggested some of the problems inherent in such a mission program. As the chronicler of the Caribbean mission, Christian Georg Andreas Oldendorp, reports:

> [Anton] added that there would always be considerable difficulties to be faced in instructing the slaves in the fundamentals of Christianity, since, on the one hand, their servitude would permit them little time for learning, and their masters would not allow it, on the other. He thought, therefore, that the goal might not be otherwise attained unless the teacher himself were a slave, since, in this manner, he would always be among them and able to instruct them unhindered.[33]

The radical suggestion that a successful missionary is one who would share the same status as those who were to be converted was in fact welcomed by both Zinzendorf and the Moravian Brethren, two of whom, Johann Leonhard Dober and Tobias Leupold, immediately volunteered to go to St. Thomas and become slaves, ignorant of the law that prevented Europeans being enslaved on that island.[34] After a year of deliberations in Herrnhut, delays caused by the Elders' skepticism about the scheme, Dober and another single brother, David Nitschmann (who had met Anton in Copenhagen), were dispatched to St. Thomas. The full story of the mission on St. Thomas has been told in detail elsewhere.[35] However, for the purposes of discussing the attitudes prevalent within the Moravian Church about the treatment and conversion of the non-Christian, there are two episodes that stand out.

One of the most astonishing occurrences during the early period of the mission on St. Thomas was the marriage of one of the German Moravian brothers, Matthias Freundlich, to a free "mulatto," Rebekka. Rebekka had originally been baptized by Roman Catholic missionaries and from the beginning of the Moravian mission had proved herself to be one of the most loyal and diligent members. The marriage between Rebekka and Matthias was originally contracted as a means to increase the two Moravian laborers' efficiency among the African and Creole congregation, most of whom were also married. However, it almost caused the demise of the Moravian mission on St. Thomas. Although the Herrnhut congregation had no objection to a European marrying a "mulatto," the European settlers on the island, led by the Reformed pastor Borm, challenged the validity of the actual marriage ceremony, claiming that the Moravian brother who had married them had not been properly ordained and thus could not administer the sacrament of marriage. Matthias and Rebekka were arrested and charged with cohabiting outside the bounds of marriage. Matthias was sentenced to a one hundred-thaler fine and lifelong penal servitude at the Danish prison of Bremerholm and Rebekka to slavery and excommunication.

33

The second remarkable occurrence was Zinzendorf's visit to St. Thomas. Appearing almost as a "deus ex machina," Zinzendorf arrived on the island on January 29, 1739,[36] and was immediately deeply moved by the number of souls (at that time around 750) who had "acquired a taste for the Gospel" on St. Thomas.

Zinzendorf's reason for traveling to St. Thomas was to see for himself the progress of the missionary movement in the Caribbean and in North America. He considered the work on St. Thomas to be more of a miracle than what was happening back in Herrnhut. But why? What was his fascination for converting these African slaves and freedmen?

Perhaps the clearest expression of Zinzendorf's motivation for this mission work can be found in his speech to the inhabitants of St. Thomas on February 15, 1739. In this speech given in Creole he clearly delineates his understanding of the natural state of sin into which the slaves have been born, their need for salvation from the inherent sinful characteristics of this slavery, the means by which they may be saved, and the political necessity of urging the slaves to remain faithful to their owners. To convert the non-Christian is both to extend the kingdom of God and to create in another instance, unique and unrepeatable, a *Vergegenwärtigung*, a making-present of Christ. This understanding of mission policy meant that baptisms were performed individually and not en masse, that the individual's path to salvation was charted by means of frequent "speakings" with spiritual helpers (such as Rebekka) from the same national background as the candidate, and that each African or Creole was a member of a small group of people who met together regularly in the evenings to discuss their spiritual growth, exchange confidences about their personal problems, encourage and forgive each other, and help each other toward Christ.

This stress on the individual nature of conversion reflected not only Zinzendorf's emphasis on the need for a personal relationship with Christ but also the necessity for the non-Christian to be completely exorcised of the "natural" attributes of his or her state of original sin. Unlike other new members of the Moravian Church, non-Christians first had to be exorcised of this evil before baptism. In his speech to the inhabitants of St. Thomas, Zinzendorf explicitly states that "the heathen cannot be naturally inclined to do as much good as a man who has been taught to do good and to avoid evil since childhood. For a heathen is accustomed to evil from his youth."[37] However, Zinzendorf considers that this "natural" inclination to evil can be overcome through conversion to Christianity. Zinzendorf, revealing his and Western society's notion of the African or Creole, maintains that baptism "remove[s] all evil thought, deceit, laziness, faithlessness, and everything that makes your condition of slavery burdensome."[38]

However, it is of the utmost importance that the listeners to this speech on the liberation of the soul realize that their physical slavery is a state created by God and thus immutable. "The Lord has made everything Himself—kings, masters, servants, and slaves. And as long as we live in this world, everyone must gladly endure the state into which God has placed him and be content with God's wise counsel."[39] The slaves are warned against expecting physical freedom after baptism (as was actually the case under Danish law in the early years of the settlement of the Danish West Indies); however, with baptism into the Moravian Church the Africans may unlearn the attributes of slavery that are sinful. Even if slavery to sin can be abolished, enslavement to the European must persist.

Zinzendorf's understanding of slavery as a God-given state of course both justified and maintained the political and economic status quo on the slave plantations of the Danish West Indies. He did not want to endanger the primary purpose of Moravian work there, the conversion of the heathen, and was well aware of the political problem that would arise if the hundreds of slaves who attended the Moravian services and wished to be baptized would also demand their physical freedom.[40]

Zinzendorf's explanation of slavery as a God-given human state thus takes on political dimensions. Although he originally leaped at Anton's suggestion that the European Moravians become slaves in order to preach the Gospel on St. Thomas, once it became clear that the mission itself would become endangered through such a contravention of Danish law, he adapted his message accordingly. In the farewell speech, as in his other writings, such as the 1747 *Homilies on the Litany of the Wounds*, Zinzendorf describes slavery as God's punishment of the Negro. It is a *Stand*, or status, as immutable in its contours as the state of marriage or being female or male.

Given that, what was Zinzendorf's understanding of race, or as he terms it "nation," that category that was just becoming current in the hierarchical classification of the human species? As did the explorer William Bosman in his *A New and Accurate Description of the Coast of Guinea* (1705), Zinzendorf believed that "God has punished the Negroes with slavery."[41] Thus, as a race the African must be enslaved although the spiritual attributes of physical slavery could be removed through baptism. The particular path toward salvation from these natural attributes of physical slavery was also determined by that "Africanness." For example, in order to understand the readiness of the soul for baptism in

Christ the Moravian missionary had to know about the spiritual and cultural background of the African candidate. For example, as David Schattschneider points out, in his *Catechism for the Heathen* (1740) Zinzendorf urged missionary workers "to pay attention to the culture of their hearers and express spiritual truths in terms and expressions which could be readily understood by the people."[42] As Zinzendorf desired the formation of indigenous churches that were fully in the hands of the local population, missionaries modeled their theology on anthropological data, in the form of the symbols and stories that had been gathered among the people, and adapted them to the Christian message.[43]

The Moravian attitude toward African slaves and freedmen was thus primarily determined by Zinzendorf's desire to spread Moravianism. He believed that God had punished the African race with slavery; Africans therefore were "naturally," that is, theologically and divinely, determined to occupy a *Stand* or status of forced servitude. However, the race or "nation" of the slave did not permanently relegate one to an inferior position within the Moravian community (as the example of Rebekka Freundlich shows). Rather, once baptized, the Black was regarded by the Moravian missionaries as a brother. Physical bondage was justified as a part of the social structure of the time; however, spiritual bondage was the mark of true slavery. As in the white man, the sinfulness of the Black lay in his or her distance from Christ. After baptism, the spiritual nature of the African was not to be distinguished from the other spiritual experiences because of one's nation but rather because of one's marital status, age, and sex. This, then, is what was expected of Andrew and Magdalene in their relations of their lives. An initial pre-Moravian condition of spiritual and physical slavery was followed by a liberation through Christ, thus effecting an entry into the white world. As we shall see, Andrew and Magdalene respond to these expectations in different ways.

Andrew and Magdalene

The audience listening to Andrew's and Magdalene's memoirs at their funerals thus expected to hear their spiritual paths outlined in a recognizable form: their African background, how they had gone to the Moravians, their growing relationship with Christ, and their role within the Moravian Church. As Africans they were expected to have been born as slaves and heathens, and to have gained to an awareness of the liberation from sin that baptism had given them. To what extent was it possible for either of these Africans to represent selfhood through the models of life writing available to them in eighteenth-century Bethlehem, that is, through the genre of the Moravian spiritual memoir (the form in which they were obliged to write their life story), and what happened to their notions of identity when they encountered those related selves?

Andrew opens his memoir, as do other Moravian writers, by giving his birthplace. "I, Andrew the Moor, was born in Iboland, in the unknown part of Africa and according to the customs of my nation was circumcised when I was 8 days old. My name was Ofodobendo Wooma" (Andrew Memoir [hereafter AM]). Iboland is, he says, in the "unknown" part of Africa. Already clearly signaling that he is an African writing for a non-African audience he marks his birthplace as unknown. In a similar compensatory gesture toward his non-African audience, when he gives his Igbo name, he uses the past tense. His present name, *Andrew the Moor*, is a label that qualifies the "I." Thus, the autograph signals his immediate alienation from his former identity. As for the other twelve Moravians of African descent who are buried in God's Acre in Bethlehem, Andrew has no family name but rather is labeled the *Moor.*

And how does Magdalene cite her origins at the beginning of her memoir? First she names her previous owner, Charles Brockden, then she gives her date of birth as the age at which she was bought by him from her previous owner. Of her childhood in Popo there is no mention. All that follows her "birth" in slavery at the age of ten is her troubled adolescence. Of this she writes, "Because my master was much concerned about the salvation of my soul and he saw that it was high time that I was protected from the temptations of the world and brought to a religious society, he suggested to me that I should go to Bethlehem" (Brockden Memoir [hereafter BM]). This Magdalene does rather unwillingly: "Because I had no desire to do so, I asked him rather to sell me to someone else, for at that time I still loved the world and desired to enjoy it fully. However, my master said to me lovingly that I should go to Bethlehem and at least try it. He knew that I would be well treated there, and if it did not suit me there, so he would take me back at any time" (BM). However, upon arrival in Bethlehem in 1743 she is welcomed with such love that she decides to stay. "In the beginning, my behavior was very bad, yes, I really tried to make them send me away again, which did not happen. The love of the brothers and sisters, however, and in particular the great mercy of the Savior which I came to feel in this time, moved me to stay here. Some time after, my master came here and gave me his permission and blessing, and I became content and happy."[44] Magdalene describes her encounter with her self as following the Moravian path. Through self-scrutiny and frequent "speakings" with the Single Sisters Choir Helper, Magdalene arrives at a consciousness of her slavery to sin. She writes: "The Savior now showed great mercy even to my poor soul, which was so deeply sunk in the slavery of sin that I never thought that I would be freed from these chains and could be admitted to grace. How happy I was therefore for the assurance, 'Also for you did Jesus Christ die on the stem of the cross, so that you might be redeemed and eternally saved.' I took this up in faith and received forgiveness of my sins" (BM). Just as Zinzendorf, the founder of the Renewed Moravian Church and originator of the practice of memoir writing, had envisaged, Magdalene's encounter with her "saved" self is one that she describes as dependent upon her *Vergegenwärtigung.* Through her faith that Christ's death is also for her sake, Magdalene is made highly conscious of Christ's presence in her life—the *Heiland* or Savior becomes a tangible partner. Although not released from her physical slavery until 1752, Magdalene writes of freeing herself from the chains of worldly sin before her reception into the congregation in 1748. Her memoir is written prior to her marriage in 1762 but after her manumission, thus dating it in the mid- to late 1750s.

Andrew's memoir is spoken in a different voice. Although we do hear of Andrew's childhood, it is not one of innocence. In his memoir he relates how, after his father's death, when he is eight, his uncle gives him as security for the loan of two goats to another man. The latter, however, does not wait to receive his goats back and sells Ofodobendo, as he was called then. What follows is a detailed description of the boy's repeated sale to traders of different West African nations until he ends up in what appears to be the house of a *Menschenfresser,* or cannibal. Locked in a room by a prospective buyer's servant, Ofodobendo becomes frightened: "I was terrified and trembled with fear, for I saw myself in a place where at least fifty heads of murdered people were hanging all around. That was the house of a cannibal, although this nation are not cannibals at all, some people eat human flesh to appear barbaric and great. I expected to be slaughtered immediately, and thought that they would have a nice appetite for me because I was young" (AM). In this "delicious" passage of Andrew's memoir, the narrative voice is not that of an older Moravian speaking of the spiritual tribulations of childhood and adolescence but rather a seasoned storyteller entertaining his audience. Andrew, the narrator of his life, is here speaking to his audience, the Moravian congregation in Bethlehem. From the stage at which his narrative breaks off, just after his owner, Thomas Noble, dies in 1747, it is clear that Andrew relates his memoir in the ensuing decade, before his marriage to Magdalene. It is likely that during the French and Indian War, which started with the attack on the Moravian Indian village of Gnadenhütten (today Lehighton), the residents of the stockaded town of Bethlehem were requested to write their memoirs in case of attack. Related in the 1750s, when Andrew is in his midtwenties and his childhood is not very distant, Andrew's story of the cannibal's house is told for non-African ears. Andrew, playing with the cultural expectations of his amanuensis and his audience, tells them of an Africa unknown to them but not to him, which they expect to and can recognize. He provides the rhetorical icing on the cake through the assertion that he expects to be slaughtered any minute because he is young and therefore tasty!—a detail almost worthy of the Brothers Grimm a hundred years later. Andrew's relation of his childhood contains consciously little that belongs to the narrative of his spiritual growth, however essential such snippets might be to a story about adventure in exotic lands.[45]

Having been rejected by his prospective "cannibal" buyer because his price is too high, Ofodobendo is sold to what appears to be a slave trader for the Europeans. Andrew relates how Ofodobendo is forced to eat pork, a meat considered unclean by the Igbo, in order not to starve. And then he enjoys the moment of first sight of the Europeans: "One morning we were scared when we saw two white people approaching us. We were certain that they were devils who wanted to fetch us" (AM). Such a reaction is justified, Andrew argues, because "we had never seen white people before and had never heard in our lives that such people existed" (AM). Reading Andrew's memoir, I can only imagine what pleasure he must have taken in relating these observations to the Laborer of the Single Brethren in Bethlehem. Made acutely aware of his race through the absence of a surname, the designation *the Moor*, attached like a patronymic to his Christian name, Andrew, the self-narrator, must have relished dictating to his German scribe his judgment of white people as devils. Furthermore, how many times must Andrew have had to hear similar reactions from Europeans to the sight of peoples of other races. For example, Maria Agnes Rothe describes her first sight of a Native American in the following fashion: "On September 22nd of that same year, in accordance with our call, we set off from Bethlehem to serve the Indian Congregation in Scheschequanick on the Susquehanna. On the journey, when I saw the first Indian face to face I was alarmed at his wild appearance."[46]

Ofodobendo's mistrust of white people is allayed only through the sight of his own people emerging from one of the ships that then carried him to Antigua. Of the Middle Passage there is no mention. Ofodobendo is sold to a Jew in New York City, who renames him after his new place—York. He is now twelve.

What does Andrew tell of York's life in the city? Like Magdalene in Philadelphia, York leads a life of worldly sin. The twelve-year-old boy roams the streets with other boys of his age and learns only "ungodly things." When his master threatens to sell him for a "pipe of wine," York turns to his neighbors to ask them for advice. Again Andrew, the narrator, reiterates the devilish nature of the non-African. He, York, the African subject, is the only one who can find a true and godly way. The neighbors teach him the Lord's Prayer and that evening York kneels down and prays: " O Lord, our neighbors say that you are very good and that you give everyone that which they ask for. If you should desire to help me find a good master in this city, then I will love you for this" (AM). Although he might be seen as tempting the Lord, York has his prayer almost answered the following day when his master offers him to Thomas Noble as payment of a loan (echoes of his Igbo days here).

In the narrative, Andrew the Moravian's voice now emerges when he refers to Thomas Noble's clerk as "Brother" Henry van Fleck. To his audience the van Flecks and the Nobles are well known, their children being in Bethlehem at that time. The teleology of the narrative is now set. York will become Andrew. But how? Mr. Noble considers York, who only a few years earlier had been good enough to eat, to be too "young and weak for his work." A second time, York when offered to Noble, is refused. In desperation York turns again to his neighbors (in what might be understood as a remnant of his Igbo past in that he relies so heavily on his community's advice), who once again recommend him to the Lord.

Andrew narrates, "I said to my unknown Lord [to whom is He unknown?] that our neighbors had described him very graciously to me and also Mr. Noble as a very good master and if He wished to so design it that I come to Mr. Noble so I would love Him forever after" (AM). The following day, York is invited to work in the Noble household for a trial period of a month and is retained. Another "Negro" is sent away.

Once owned by Noble, York had frequent contact with the Moravian Brethren in New York and probably met Zinzendorf himself when he stayed with the Nobles. Andrew tells how the young adolescent hears the Moravians talk of how "the Savior had spilt his blood for me and all black people and that he loved both me and all others just as much as the white people, which I did not believe, but rather thought that God only loved those people who were eminent figures and possessed great wealth" (AM). Now that Andrew's narrative assumes the voice of the Moravian memoirist—whether German peasant, artisan, or nobleman—the young person hides away to read the Gospel, away from the temptations of the world. York learns to read quickly and keeps a book by him all the time in his sack. Unlike the other young Moravians, however, York does not join the Noble family in their evening prayers, but rather, "I crept away to a corner, went up to my room and prayed and did as I had seen and heard them do" (AM). Why does York not pray with the family? Because he still does not believe that his prayers are in the same language as those of the white people. Even after the lady of the house has invited him to join the family in their prayers "because the Savior died for me as much as for them" York still goes to his room to repeat his prayers in his own way (AM).

York's double life of public good works and secret consciousness of sin is almost too much for him, and he resolves to commit suicide by throwing himself out of a window. Although the devil has stood behind him on all too many occasions, this time as he is standing in the window: "it seemed to me as if someone were pulling me back and I came to my senses" (AM). From that moment on York encounters his Moravian self—his language of consciousness of religion and sinfulness is that of the Moravian Church. He, as do all other members of the congregation, recognizes his unworthiness and poverty in the face of the Savior's "meritorious sufferings" and desires nothing but to become a member of the Moravian Brethren. Although George Whitefield offers to baptize him, Mr. Noble says no and allows him rather to go to Bethlehem in 1745. After various speakings with Brother Nathaniel Seidel (the Laborer of the Single Brethren at that time), he stays in Bethlehem and is baptized Andrew in the presence of Mr. Noble on February 15, 1746. (In the memoir an editorial note points out that Andrew was the first Negro to be baptized by the Moravians in Pennsylvania.) What follows is the Moravian Andrew's voice, mingled with hundreds of other voices in the congregation who, regardless of their race or gender, speak of their communion with the Brethren "as impossible to describe." It is at this point that Andrew's narrative breaks off and the amanuensis adds the following information about his walk through life with the Bethlehem congregation: "Our late brother walked a blessed and edifying path in the Congregation and it was a true pleasure for him to speak of the Savior to any poor black whenever he could. He likes to describe what the Savior had done in his heart, [and then added in a footnote] and his election by grace to have come out of the darkness into light and the power of Satan to God and to the congregation of believers, all this was great and important to him" (AM). The editor continues, "In his outward affairs he was loyal and hard-working" (Andrew appears to have worked as a day laborer). Of Andrew's faith the narrator assures the audience that "his end showed that he believed"(AM).

Encountered Selves

Writing on Frederick Douglass's last diary entry in which he records a visit to the last surviving member of the family that owned him in order to discover more about his birth, Henry Louis Gates observes: "A sense of self as we have defined it in the West since the Enlightenment turns in part upon written records. Most fundamentally, we mark a human being's existence by his or her birth and death dates, engraved in granite on every tombstone. Our idea of self, it is fair to argue, is as inextricably interwoven with our ideas of time as it is with uses of language.... Slavery's time was delineated by memory and memory alone."[47]

As I have tried to show in this chapter, the Moravian notion of selfhood certainly fits Gates's description of the Enlightenment's definition of self-consciousness through literacy. In the endless speakings and writings about the self, Moravians were familiar with the textuality of life. Each person dated him- or herself, named his or her parentage and home, and used memory of the past to fashion a picture of the soul by which he or she wished to be remembered. The Moravian memoir was designed to be the history of the church, a history of identifying stories. But not all the writing subjects could supply those Enlightenment prerequisites of selfhood, namely, literacy and origin. Magdalene can provide neither her date of birth, parentage, nor place of birth. (These I actually identified from her manumission document, her origins as given by her owner.) In Magdalene's brief account of her life until her midtwenties we hear a voice telling the Moravian audience who knows that she was in slavery that in her opinion her true slavery was to sin and not as a slave to Charles Brockden. By preferring a life of bondage to a life of salvation Magdalene, in the narrative of her life, recounts how she was losing her self. Brockden, her owner, was also concerned at the state of her soul, for when she went to Bethlehem he manumitted her only provisionally, saying that if she were to leave the Brethren that he would rescind his manumission and take her back to protect her from the sins of the world. In 1758, he is convinced enough of her commitment to the congregation finally to manumit her. She does not mention her seventeen-year marriage to Andrew or her three dead children. Her almost ninety years of life are marked only by a three-page memoir, a gravestone, and the occasional mention in the accounts of the congregation.[48]

Andrew, however, provides us with a much richer narrative of his life, a life that switches from Africa, to New York, to Bethlehem. With his locale, Andrew's voice switches, too. Relating his life to a Moravian brother when he is also in his midtwenties, Andrew plays with his audience. His spiritual narrative begins, as Equiano's twenty-five years later, with his childhood experiences. His Igbo name, *Ofodobendo,* meaning "May righteousness guide my life," is clearly and accurately remembered. His peregrinations, like those of young Joseph in the Bible, tell of narrow escapes and frequent selling into slavery. Andrew, narrating Ofodobendo, is well versed in Bible stories. Maybe he, too, as does Equiano, wishes to draw the parallel between his Igbo nation and the Jewish people? But once he is owned by a Jew in New York, that identification changes and he likens himself to the Christians—the Moravians—although he keeps himself separate in his communication with God. Always aware of his alienation from the white people, perhaps never quite getting over the thought that they are of the devil, York/Andrew maintains his own personal relationship with his Savior—a Moravian thing to do.

Andrew writes more of his memory and to great effect. Knowing the stories he is supposed to relate, of spiritual growth and awakening, Andrew uses the tropes of the Moravian memoir to tell a story that is uniquely his, a story that is so memorable in the Moravian community in Bethlehem that visiting anthropologists are sent to him to record data on his African nation. As does so much of African and African-American literature since, Andrew's story becomes a representative account of an Igbo's life. But I would argue that Andrew's story remains his: one cleverly wrought to meet expectations, to turn tropes—signifyin', as Gates would call it, on the dominant tropes of Moravian religious language.

The Memoir of Andrew
(?–1779)

The late brother, Andrew the Moor, has dictated the following about his life:[49]

I, Andrew the Moor, was born in Ibo land in the unknown part of Africa and was circumcised according to the custom of my nation when I was eight days old. My name was Ofodobendo Wòoma. My father died when I was about eight years old and my brother, who himself had five children and was poor, took me in. However, not long afterwards he borrowed two goats from a man for two years and gave me to him as a security, that when he received the goats back he should return me. However, he did not wait for this to happen but rather lay a pipe of tobacco in my path so that I stepped on it and broke it and this he took as a reason to sell me to someone else after a year had passed.

In the space of a short time I was often sold and resold and came from one nation to another whose language I did not understand until I was brought to a large area called Nemils where a merchant of that country bought me, clothed me, and took me into his house with his servant. A few weeks later on orders from his master the servant took me to a house not too far away. Once I was in the house I was immediately locked in. I was terrified and trembled with fear, for I saw myself in a place where at least 50 heads of murdered people were hanging all around. That was the house of a cannibal, although this nation are not cannibals at all, some people eat human flesh to appear barbaric and great. I expected to be slaughtered immediately, and thought that they would have a nice appetite for me because I was young. My companion however demanded more for me than they wanted to give and thus he took me back with him, brought me once again to the aforementioned area, there took my clothes and sold me to a man who traded upcountry.

I was immediately taken onto a wagon with a number of others whose language I did not understand; that pained me greatly, until I found a girl from my country who comforted me greatly. For the first three or four days they gave me nothing to eat or drink but pork, which it is forbidden to eat in my country. Whoever eats pork is hated and shunned by others as a very evil person. Because I was almost starved I was eventually forced to eat a little of it.

We were brought to the coast of Guinea and the girl and I kept together and waited to see what would happen to us. One morning we were terribly scared when we saw two white people coming towards us. We were certain that they were of the devil and had come to fetch us, because we had never seen a white person before and had never in our lives heard that such people existed. One of them, the Captain of a ship, waved to us that we should follow him, which we did with great fear, and we were taken onto the ship where we saw three or four Negroes and expected to be killed any minute. However, as the ship's hold was opened and about sixty black people came out, our fear disappeared and I comforted myself with the thought that I would fare as they had.

We were taken to Antigua where I was sold with about thirty others to a Captain from New York who sold me in New York to a Jew, who named me York. That was in 1741 and I was about twelve years old then. During the first year I had nothing to do but to run about the streets with other boys, where I learned many godless ways. During the second year my master wanted to sell me to Madeira for a pipe of wine. I was very concerned about this, told a few neighbors and asked for their advice. They said that they were unable to help me, but that I should ask God to help me. I asked how I should pray and what I should pray for. They taught me the Lord's Prayer. In the evening I knelt down and said: "Oh Lord, our neighbors say that you are very good and that you give everybody what they ask for from you. If you wish to help me to a good master in this city I will love you greatly for that." The next day my master offered me to Mr. Noble, to whom he was in debt and Brother Henry van Fleck (his Clerk or apprentice) fetched me. To my great disappointment Mr. Noble did not want me because I appeared to be too young and weak for his work.

After I had been brought to him for a second time and had been refused again for that reason I told my neighbors that Mr. Noble had an inclination to buy me if I were stronger. To this they replied, that there was no better man in New York than he and that I should pray to the Lord to make him so disposed that he would buy me. This I did that evening and said to my unknown Lord that our neighbors had described Him to me once again very graciously and had described Mr. Noble as a very good master and that if He wanted to bring it to pass that I should come to Mr. Noble so I would love Him forever. The following day I was brought to Mr. Noble's house with another Negro boy for a trial period of four weeks. At the end of the same the other boy was sent back and I was bought by Mr. Noble.

At this time the first [Moravian] brethren came to New York and lodged with Mr. Noble. They often said to me that our Savior had spilt His blood for me and all black people and that He loved me and all [black people] just as much as the white people, which I did not believe but rather thought that God loved only those people who had cut a figure in the world, possessed riches, etc. However, I did resolve to find out where possible whether or not what I had so often heard from the brothers was true. Mr. Noble sent me to school and because I was very eager, I learned to read in less than six months. From that time forward I always had the New Testament or another good book in my sack and read from them whenever I had time and opportunity to do so. Mr. Noble held prayers with his family every morning and evening and although I was quite often in the same room I never prayed with them but rather crept into a corner and then went into my room and prayed and acted as I had seen and heard them act, until one time Mrs. Noble said that, because the Savior had suffered and died for me as well as for them, I could be as blessed as they and I should pray with them which I then did. I always repeated it however when I was alone in my room.

I was very anxious about my salvation and attempted to gain it through my own abilities. In the mornings according to my master's admonition I often undertook to do my work that day happily, to deal with everyone with love and constantly to pray, but unfortunately something often would happen straight after the resolution that made this goal unattainable and cast me into a state of fear such that I did not trust myself to pray again until the next day when I hoped that the Lord would have forgotten my behavior. While praying in my room such a fear overcame me that I thought that the Devil was standing behind me. Once, when I had become tired of this hard and wearisome way to salvation and saw no possibility of attaining my goal I resolved to throw myself out of a window and in this way to put an end to my sinful life. I was already standing in the opening and preparing to make the jump when it seemed as though someone was pulling me back. At this I came to my senses and asked the Lord for forgiveness amidst a thousand tears.

From this day forth I was made aware of my unworthiness and incapacity daily and the Savior's love and mercy and His meritorious suffering and death made such an impression on my heart that I wished for nothing so much as to become a true merit of Jesus' pain and also a member of the Brethren's Congregation. I often had a desire to be baptized and once Mr. Whitefield offered to baptize me himself. But Mr. Noble refused. At the end of 1745 Mr. Noble allowed me to go to Bethlehem where I arrived with a happy heart on January 9, 1746 in the company of the Brothers

William Edmonds and John Hopson. I had various blessed talks with Brother Nathaniel and revealed to him my whole heart. A few weeks after I came here, Mr. Noble (my master) (who had given me to Brother Spangenberg) also came to Bethlehem to a synod. On February 15, during his stay, I was baptized in Jesus' death by Brother Christian Rauch and named Andrew (he was the first Negro the Brethren baptized in Pennsylvania). It is impossible for me to describe the blessedness of my heart that I felt during this. The following Sabbath I had the great grace to enjoy the body and blood of my dear Saviour in the Holy Sacrament with the congregation. In April of the same year I returned to New York to serve Mr. Noble during his illness and after his death I returned to my dear Bethlehem. Thus far his report.

In 1762 on January 21 he was joined to the now widow, Magdalene, in holy matrimony which the dear Saviour blessed with three children of whom only one little son, Andrew, stayed in this mortal life a short while. Our late Brother led a blessed and edifying life in the congregation and it was a true pleasure for him to tell a poor black person about the Saviour whenever he could. He liked to recount what the Saviour had done for his soul (and his election by grace, that he had come out of the darkness into light, from the power of Satan to God and to the Congregation of believers, was very great and important to him.) In his external affairs he was loyal and diligent. For some years he had been afflicted with a heavy cough. His desire to be at home with the Lord finally became so strong that he could hardly wait for the blessed little hour and often sighed, "O my dear Saviour, o come soon and fetch me." But he was very patient and relaxed. On the 13th in the evening he departed very gently and his end showed that he was a believer.

The Memoir of Magdalene Beulah Brockden (1731–1820)

Our Negro sister Magdalena, who happily departed on January on January 3rd of this year, left behind the following report.

I was known, a slave or the property of the late Mr. Brockden who bought me from another master, when I was ten years old and from then on I served his family until I was grown. Because my master was much concerned about the salvation of my soul and he saw that it was high time that I was protected from the temptations of the world and brought to a religious society, so he suggested to me that I should go to Bethlehem.

Because I had no desire to do so, I asked him rather to sell me to someone else, for at that time I still loved the world and desired to enjoy it fully. However, my master said to me lovingly that I should go to Bethlehem and at least try it. He knew that I would be well treated there. And if it did not suit me there so he would take me back at any time. When I arrived here I was received with such love and friendship by the official workers and all the Brethren that I was much ashamed. (She arrived on November 23, 1743 in Bethlehem.) I soon received permission to remain here. My behaviour in the beginning was so bad; I really tried to be sent away again, which did not happen. The love of the Brethren, however, and in particular the great mercy of the Saviour that I came to feel at this time moved me to stay here. Some time after, my master came here and gave me his permission and blessing, and I become content and happy.

The Saviour showed great mercy to me poor soul, which was so deeply sunk in the slavery of sin that I never thought that I would be freed from these chains and could receive grace. How happy I was for the words, "Also for you did Jesus die on the stem of the cross so that you may be redeemed and eternally blessed." I understood this in faith and received forgiveness for my sins.

In 1748 on the 19th May she was baptized in the death of Jesus and on the 26th January 1749 she attained the pleasure of Holy Communion with the congregation. On 21st January 1762 she entered into matrimony with the Negro Brother Andrew, and this marriage was blessed with two sons who have both gone home. In 1779 on March 30th she became a widow. She enjoyed lasting health until her old age. About fourteen days ago she became seriously ill, and it soon became clear that this illness was to be her end, and this became clear to her also. She fell asleep the above day in the 89th year of her life.

Notes

1. "Andrew the Moor" (?–1779) and "Magdalene Beulah Brockden" (1731–1820), memoirs, MSS, Moravian Archives, Bethlehem Pennsylvania, hereafter abbreviated MAB. Magdalene's memoir exists in both English and German. The cited version is my translation of the German version.

Andrew's memoir was written in German. All manuscript sources for this article are written in German script. Special training is required to read these manuscripts—even for native German speakers. A two-week script seminar is held every summer at the Moravian Archives in Bethlehem, Pennsylvania, for those who wish to acquire this skill.

2. For a historical discussion of Andrew's memoir with translation, see Daniel B. Thorp, "Chattel with a Soul: The Autobiography of a Moravian Slave," *Pennsylvania Magazine of History and Biography* 112 (1988): 433–51.

3. Anna Boehler, memoir, MS, MAB.

4. Paul Münster, memoir, MS, MAB.

5. Andrew the Moor, memoir, MS, MAB.

6. Magdalene Beulah Brockden, memoir, MS, MAB.

7. S. E. Ogude, *Genuis in Bondage: The Study of the Origins of African Literature in English* (Ile-Ife, Nigeria: University of Ife Press, 1983), 120.

8. Georges Gusdorf, "Conditions and Limits of Autobiography," in *Autobiography: Essays Theoretical and Critical*, ed. James Olney, 28–48 (Princeton, NJ: Princeton University Press, 1980).

9. M. Mason, "The Other Voice: Autobiography of Women Writers," ibid., 207–35; Patrician Meyer Spacks, "Female Rhetoric," *The Private Self: Theory and Practice of Women's Autobiographical Writings*, ed. S. Benstock, 177–91 (Chapel Hill: University of North Carolina Press, 1988); E. Jelinek, *The Tradition of Women's Autobiography: From Antiquity to the Present* (Boston: Twayne, 1986); C. Heilbrun, *Writing a Woman's Life* (New York: Norton, 1988).

10. Mason, "The Other Voice," 210.

11. S. S. Friedman, "Women's Autobiographical Selves: Theory and Practice"; Benstock, *The Private Self*, 34–62, here at p. 45. I have explored elsewhere the extent to which this passivity in the process of self-differentiation is the only acceptable notion of selfhood for a Moravian woman in the eighteenth century. See Katherine M. Faull, "The American *lebenslauf*: Women's Autobiography from Eighteenth-Century Moravian Bethlehem, Pennsylvania," *Yearbook of the Society for German-American Studies* 27 (1992): 23–48.

12. R. B. Stepto, *From behind the Veil: A Study of Afro-American Narrative* (Urbana: University of Illinois Press, 1979), 8.

13. Phillis Wheatley, *Poems on Various Subjects, Religious and Moral by Phillis Wheatley* (London, 1773).

14. Frederick Douglass, *Narrative of the Life of an American Slave of 1845* (n.p., n.d.).

15. Ogude, *Genius in Bondage*, 7. See H. L. Gates, Jr.'s extended discussion of this issue in his two volumes, *Figures in Black: Words, Signs, and the "Racial" Self* (Oxford: Oxford University Press, 1989) and *The Signifying Monkey: A Theory of Afro-American Literary Criticism* (New York: Oxford University Press, 1988). *Figures in Black* explores the extent to which literacy was the defining characteristic of humanity for eighteenth- and nineteenth-century Western thinkers and was thus a necessary attribute of any African or African American who wished to be recognized as human in the West. In *The Signifying Monkey*, Gates develops further the African American critical tradition in twentieth-century literature and culture. "Signifyin'," according to Gates, consists of the textual strategy of turning tropes on the "white man's idiom" through a process of reversal, repetition, and amplification. Thus, having learned the white man's written idiom, the African or African American author then uses that knowledge to signify his or her difference from that idiom through the text.

16. John Marrant, *A Narrative of the Lord's Wonderful Dealings with John Marrant, a Black (Now going to Preach the Gospel in Nova Scotia) Born in New York, in North America: Taken Down from his own relation, Arranged, Corrected, and Published by the Reverend Mr. Aldridge* (London: by the Author, 1785).

17. Ottobah Cuguano, *Thoughts and Sentiments on the Evil of Slavery* (London: for the Author, 1787).

18. Olaudah Equiano, *The Interesting Narrative of the Life of Olaudah Equiano or Gustavus Vassa, the African, written by Himself* (London: for the Author, 1789).

19. Gates, *Figures in Black*, 115.

20. C. Obianju Acholonu, *The Igbo Roots of Olaudah Equiano* (Owerri, Nigeria: Afa, 1989).

21. S. E. Ogude, "Facts into Fiction: Equiano's Narrative Reconsidered," *Research in African Literatures* 13 (1982): 31–43.

22. E. Isichei, "The Life of Olaudah Equiano or Gustavus Vassa the African" and "The Igbo Roots of Olaudah Equiano" (book review) *Journal of African History* 33 (1992): 164–65. For her earlier uses of Equiano's text, see her *The Ibo People and the Europeans* (New York: St. Martin's Press, 1973). Large portions of Equiano's descriptions of his native Igboland are actually almost verbatim quotations from Anthony Benezet, *Some Historical Account of Guinea . . .* (1771). Benezet, a Philadelphian Quaker and associate of Charles Brockden (Magdalene's owner), made up his own text for this influential antislavery tract with extended quotations from extant printed sources by European explorers and interviews conducted with newly arrived African slaves on the quayside in Philadelphia. Benezet's two sisters, Judith and Susanna, were actually members of the Moravian community in Bethlehem from the early 1740s and lived with Magdalene in the Single Sisters Choir.

23. K. Orban, "Dominant and Submerged Discourses in *The Life of Olaudah Equiano* (or Gustavus Vassa?)," *African American Review* 27 (1993): 655–64.

24. S. Marren, "Between Slavery and Freedom: The Transgressive Self in Olaudah Equiano's Autobiography," *PMLA* 108 (1993): 94–106.

25. C. Pedersen, "Middle Passages: Representations of the Slave Trade in Caribbean and African American Literature," *The Massachusetts Review* 34 (1993): 225–38.

26. G. Murphy, "Olaudah Equiano: Accidental Tourist," *Eighteenth Century Studies* 27 (1994): 551–68.

27. For a collection of Moravian memoirs, see Katherine M. Faull, *Moravian Women's Memoirs: Their Related Lives 1750–1820* (Syracuse, NY: Syracuse University Press, 1997).

28. For details, see "A Very Dark Genealogy" (Notes and Queries) *Pennsylvania Magazine of History and Biography* 29 (1905): 363–65. Although this note claims that both Andrew and Magdalene were given their freedom after entering the Moravian community (albeit some years later) there is no evidence that Andrew was ever manumitted by the trustees of the community. There is no manumission document for Andrew in the Moravian Archives. Thorp also maintains that Andrew remained the property of the community until his death (see Thorp, "Chattel with a Soul," 434).

29. By all accounts, Zinzendorf's grandmother read Ziegenbalg and Plütschau's mission reports to him as a child. Later, while a pupil at Francke's Pedagogium, Zinzendorf actually met these two missionaries. See Nikolaus Ludwig von Zinzendorf, *Texte zur Mission*, ed. Helmut Bintz (Hamburg: Friedrich Wittig, 1979), 37.

30. As quoted in Zinzendorf, *Texte zur Mission*, 37.

31. While a whole essay could be devoted to the history of the mission on St. Thomas, for the purposes

of this article I will draw briefly on the excellent translation available in C. G. A. Oldendrop, *History of the Mission of the Evangelical Brethren on the Caribbean Islands of St. Thomas, St. Croix, and St. John*, ed. J. J. Bossard, trans. A. R. Highfield and V. Barac (Ann Arbor, MI: Karoma, 1987).

32. Ibid., 271.

33. Ibid., 271.

34. Ibid., 272.

35. Oldendorp, *Caribbean Islands.*

36. Zinzendorf was actually unaware of the plight of the imprisoned Moravians. However, after an appeal to the governor, Matthias and Rebekka Freundlich were released, ostensibly to aid Zinzendorf in his work there.

37. Ibid., 362.

38. Ibid., 363.

39. Ibid.

40. Zinzendorf had been aware of the potential problems caused by the mission work on St. Thomas for quite some time. See, for example, his 1736 instructions to the Moravian missionaries to the Samoyed, "Under no circumstances involve yourself in external affairs other than work. The Brethren on St. Thomas are teaching the Moors to write, we disapprove of this completely. One can arouse the anger of the authorities with such a small thing." Otto Uttendörfer, *Die Wichtigsten Missionsinstruktionen Zinzendorfs* (Herrnhut: Verlag der Missionsbuchhandlung, 1913), 9.

41. Oldendorp, *Caribbean Islands*, 363. On God's original "punishment" of the Africans, see '*Race,*' *Writing and Difference*, ed. H. L. Gates Jr. (Chicago: University of Chicago Press, 1986), 10. As a source, Gates quotes William Bosman, *A New and Accurate Description of the Coast of Guinea* (1705; repr., London, 1967), 146, 147. Benezet also quotes Bosman at length.

42. D. Schattschneider, "The Missionary Theologies of Zinzendorf and Spangenberg," *Transactions of the Moravian Historical Society* 22 (1975): 213–33, here p. 12.

43. In the early mission this information was provided by national helpers, who were from the various African nations represented among the slaves such as the Igbo, Mandingo, and Papaa. In the records of the Caribbean missions, the Moravians were most particular in noting down the African nation of origin of each member of the Moravian mission in the Caribbean, along with the original name, the slave name, and the baptized name. After baptism, the African nation of origin usually decreased in significance (although it seems not to be the case with Andrew), and the specific nation is rarely mentioned.

44. Magdalene's manumission document is dated March 3, 1752. It is written with the proviso that Brockden may rescind that manumission at any time if he sees that Magdalene might be in danger.

45. This striking passage in Andrew's story reappears in Oldendorp's anthropological account of the Igbo. Oldendorp writes, "[They] possess a vast land which lies in the interior of Africa, as I was told by one Negro of this nation, with whom I had spoken in Pennsylvania" (Oldendorp, *Caribbean Islands*, 167). A few pages later, in a section on cannibalism, he writes, "An Ibo assured me that the elite of the Okwa nation eat human flesh for the sake of its good taste" (ibid., 179). How do we know the source is Andrew? Oldendorp continues, "He had been led through their land as a prisoner, and, as he said, he saw with no little horror and fear about fifty human heads hanging on the walls of one house" (ibid.). As we can see, Andrew's story has changed somewhat. Rather than that the people (whom in his memoir he does not identify) eat human flesh just to appear bar-

barous now he ascribes to them an appetite for human flesh based on its flavor. Andrew's story now becomes an identifying story for all Okwa.

46. Maria Agnes Rothe, memoir, MS, MAB.

47. Gates, *Figures in Black*, 100.

48. There is actually one mention of Magdalene in the minutes of the Elders' Conference for July 30, 1764. *Conferenz-Protocoll der Committee in Bethlehem von 1762 bis May 1780*, entry for July 30, 1764, MS, MAB.

49. Another translation of Andrew's memoir can be found in "Chattel with a Soul: The Autobiography of a Moravian Slave," *Pennsylvania Magazine of History and Biography*, 112 (July 1988): 433–51. The original German memoir is to be found in the Moravian Archives, Bethlehem, Pa.

The Eighteenth-Century Black Wor(l)d and Early Writers' Biblical Literacy

EIGHTEENTH-CENTURY AFRO-BRITISH-AMERICAN WRITERS WERE possessed of a great deal of biblical literacy. Indeed, their exposure to a wide breadth of methods and paradigms for interpretation is indicative of the depth of their understanding of the complex layers of biblical truths, connotations, and denotations of the Word. Furthermore, their awareness of the range of implications the Bible held for their existence—in secular, sacred, political, individual, and social contexts—was equally immense. Regrettably, as John Saillant observes, modern scholarship's failure to "incorporate the biblicism of early black Christianity" has contributed to an essentialized view of the history of "early African-American Christianity" as originating in the "emotion, expression and movement" of "the post-revolutionary expansion of evangelical Arminianism," to the exclusion of "those [Black Christians] who were [also] theologically sophisticated" and grounded in Calvinist "doctrine, theology, and text."[1] The latter "more inclusive" (emotionally and intellectually inspired) view has important implications for our consideration of early Black writers' biblical literacy, as it helps to establish the grounds on which we interpret eighteenth-century Afro-British-American literature.

Increasingly, the emphasis on the value of Black biblical studies in recent literary scholarship has given us important keys for understanding the impact of religion on the study of eighteenth-century black texts.[2] Undeniably, studies of plantation cultures and enslaved African-Americans' integration of oral and written African spiritual traditions with Western biblical ones have been critical to our understanding of the inextricable relationship between the Word, the Black world, and Black letters in the New World(s) from the very beginning. However, the value of religion as a rich source from which a developing Black consciousness and Black aesthetic can be seen to emerge in eighteenth-century Black letters has evinced yet another quandary.

Specifically, for writers like Jupiter Hammon, Phillis Wheatley, James Albert Gronniosaw, John Marrant, and Olaudah Equiano, "religion indeed has produced"[3] a context within which their works are interpreted less as a testament to their mastery of sacred and secular texts, and more as an emblem of an era of a passive regressive literary legacy out of which African-American literature has (progressively) evolved. Two important considerations emerge: first, because these early writers are considered neither "authentically" Black enough by twenti-eth- and twenty-first-century aesthetic standards, nor "traditionally" American or British enough by eighteenth-century standards, they are often either entirely omitted from Anglo/African-American survey courses and anthologies or included as an afterthought, token representative, or place marker for diversity, without sufficient attention given to such formal elements as early Black writers' mastery of extended biblical exegeses.[4]

For example, while selections from Wheatley's works might be marginally included in courses on women's, African-American, American, and perhaps even postcolonial or British (Black Atlantic) literature, such inclusions typically serve as (independent or intersecting) markers of race, gender, or class. As a consequence, rarely does one find a concentrated study of her body of works in, say, a course dedicated to major writers or genres, much less a course devoted entirely to the life and letters of this great Afro-British-American poet. Further, the omission of writers such as Briton Hammon, Gronniosaw, Marrant, Equiano, and Venture Smith from early Anglo and African-American autobiography courses is equally puzzling. Clearly, the introduction and exploration of alternative Black narrative forms such as conversion, captivity, and spir-

itual autobiography can only enrich Anglo and African-American studies. Admittedly, the lack of necessary comprehensive texts poses some
difficulties as those of us who courageously tackle these exciting and
dynamic areas are well aware. For example, one requires at least three,
perhaps more, anthologies as well as extensive supplemental material
(usually in the form of large and typically expensive course packets) to
support a substantive course in early Black spiritual autobiography.
Moreover, one must undertake the labor-intensive act of pedagogical
exorcism required to undo the damage caused by the categorization of all
Black autobiography before the Reconstruction as "slave narratives."
Evidence of this prevailing point of view can be illustrated by the fact
that no single anthology to date includes all the unabridged works of
even the relatively small canon of "well-known" eighteenth-century
Afro-British-American literary figures, let alone the inclusion of any
accompanying comprehensive introductory biographical, historical, or
critical summaries of early Black spiritual writings—reminiscent of those
we have become accustomed to seeing in Bedford, Norton, and Riverside collections.[5]

Curiously, while the wave of anthologizing contemporary Black
literature and criticism continues to flourish, there has been insufficient
expansion in terms of historical and "cultural" depth and breadth. Notice-
ably, serious integration of primary and secondary works and sources into
useful collections for course study in early religious literature—Puritan
elegies, conversion narratives, sermons, meditations, letters, and other
forms of spiritual writing by early Black writers—remains lacking. Such is
the case, despite the overwhelming scholarly editions, published critical
essays, short anthologies, dissertations, and other texts (published and
unpublished) in this and closely related fields and disciplines, suggesting
there is a wealth of information about early Black writers' biblical literacy
to be gleaned from such resources. For example, Wheatley's neoclassical
work is as much a reflection of her biblical literacy as are her Puritan
elegies. Imagine, for example, what the designing and compiling of an
anthology that would draw together the "Brothers and Sisters of the
Spirit" from Briton Hammon to Amanda Berry Smith or Maria Stewart[6]
would mean for early Black autobiography studies. The potential for the
expansion of our interrogation and analysis of Christianity, race and gen-

der, and spirituality in antebellum religious literature, as well as the inter-disciplinary possibilities are nearly boundless.

The second consideration that emerges as result of deprecatory views of early black literature as a religious production is the myopic expectation that there is little left to be explored beyond highlighting early Black writers' use of Christian rhetoric to argue against oppression and slavery. To be sure, scholarship has not yet fully explored all trajec-tories with regard to early Black Christian modes of subtle protest and related African significatory practices. Radically, new trends in literary scholarship celebrate, rather than defend, the work of early Black writ-ers as religious productions. Specifically, all of these authors' extensions of the concept of redemption to argue for their spiritual and material rights demonstrate the value of metaphor in their use of biblical lan-guage to overturn or subvert negative connotations of the meaning of blackness as it is applied to people of African descent. Namely, early Black writers used Scripture to expose figurative connotations of famil-ial, national, and cultural unity as being symbolically and simultane-ously dependent upon concepts of the alien, foreigner, outcast, or other. In this manner, their writings consciously reconstruct and thereby attempt mimetic racial and cultural reunification of the Christian family of Black and white believers connected through the symbolism of blood. Hence, their works function as more than mere inscriptions of Black humanity; these interpretive emanations produce scriptural indictments that hold the white Christian (and slaveholding) world accountable to the spirit, letter, and truth of the Word. In so doing, early Black writers, building on the strength of their biblical literacy and mastery, write themselves back into the Book of Life.[7]

Thus, their intricate exegeses rest on two interrelated and inextri-cably linked scriptural themes brought forth either directly or indirectly in early Black writings: blood and redemption. Two frequently cited New Testament passages that exemplify the biblical connections to these central themes are "And [God] hath made of one blood all nations of men for to dwell on all the face of the earth, and hath determined the times before appointed, and the bounds of their habitation"[8] and "In whom we have redemption through his blood, even the forgiveness of sins."[9] The first scripture is taken from Paul's sermon to unbelievers in the city of Athens about God's divine authority, presence, power, and preeminence. Here in Athens, Paul issues a call for repentance, especially of the worship of false gods, and for man's hubris in assuming that God exists as an ornament and design of man. Further, Paul issues a warning that as judgment day approaches the return of Jesus—mankind's redeemer and judge—is eminent. The second scripture echoes similar themes within the familial language of God the "Father" as ultimate creator who has "redeemed" humanity through the "blood" of his "dear son."[10] Importantly, early Black writers demonstrate a level of biblical interpretation and analysis beyond mere attainment or mastery of literacy. Namely, the trope of the talking book that signifies the relationship of orality to literacy through Black intertextuality is further complicated by the literate African's mastery of the Bible as a sacred text that has been symbolically marked by an extended interpretive language with which to speak. While these two scriptures convey a wealth of interpretative strategies and scriptural translations, a few snapshots later of the ways that scholarship has celebrated aspects of the literature that religion has produced demonstrate the value of early Black biblical literacy.

"Redemption neither sought nor knew"[11] was a notion that Wheatley's journey from "Africa to America" underscored. First purchased by John Wheatley as a servant and companion for his wife, Susanna, she later gains the full knowledge of her spiritual purchase by the "redeeming blood" of Jesus Christ.[12] Despite Julian Mason's reminder that Wheatley's "was an education that would have been prized in many a Boston family, even among its elite; . . . supplemented by contact with persons of status and education, . . . particularly ministers, who tended to encourage her religious, intellectual, and literary development,"[13] he condescendingly, if respectfully, paints her as gifted master "craftsman . . . concerned with . . . taking a given or obvious topic and fitting it skillfully to an already existing pattern" (14). In this regard, however, he points precisely to "the strongest influences on her work . . . religion [and] the Bible."[14] Perhaps, it might be helpful to consider Wheatley's poetic transformations in the same way one regards the speeches and sermons of preachers and biblical scholars. From contemporary Methodist ministers like John Whitefield, Lemuel Haynes, and Marrant to such modern religious figures as Martin Luther King Jr.

and Cornel West, Wheatley's poetry also demonstrates the gift for taking the most mundane of topics and fashioning them into elaborate divinely inspired narratives of nearly liturgical magnitude. It is precisely her sincere religious commitment, coupled with her intellectual and artistic dexterity, that makes the "mood and the message of her poem to the University of Cambridge sound as if might have been issued from the pulpit."[15] Indeed, it might be interesting to think about what it would mean to include Wheatley's exhortations, along with works by Francis Harper, Maria Stewart, and even Jarena Lee as yet another form of an early Black woman's sermonic tradition. There can be no doubt that for this devout and pious young Christian woman religion indeed had greatly inspired the evangelical thrust that Mason and others recognized in her works. However, her knowledge of "select standard eighteenth-century Protestant commentaries on Scripture and . . . approved secular applications of biblical passages"[16] had an equally commanding effect on her mastery of biblical paraphrase in her occasional and neo-classical poetry. Such biblical literacy is similarly reflected in her ability to extend, suspend, and then release the tension between empathetic and celebratory urgings in her elegiac voice. As do "Mary Magdalene and the other Mary"[17] departing the sepulcher, the Christian Wheatley proclaims the unbounded joys of heaven to the earthbound mourners, as the African Wheatley celebrates in verse a redemptive return to spiritual and physical Eden through divinely inspired biblical inscriptions on her heart and mind and "Gambia on [her] soul."[18]

In his sermonic missive it is not only of "Christ's redeeming blood"[19] that Jupiter Hammon intertextually instructs Wheatley. Certainly, Hammon is aware of the biblical meaning of the Savior's blood, which spiritually redeemed both him and Wheatley. He also knows "the term was used . . . to establish work agreements between employers and employees, particularly . . . the white indentured . . . referred to as 'redemptioneers.' "[20] Moreover, his reference to her as a "pious *youth*" reminds that he intends to refer to spiritual and physical freedom. Recall that in his 1787 "Address to the Negroes of New York" Hammon states that he "should be glad if other, especially the *young* Negroes, were to be free."[21] What is most significant about Hammon's mastery of biblical language, like Wheatley's paraphrase, is the knowledge and ease with which he manipulates Scripture and common biblical language simultaneously to connote encoded meaning for his Black audiences and to critique directly (preach or otherwise give lessons to) a white slaveholding society that tolerated and permitted him to do so because he does so within the confines of authorized biblical frameworks and language. In this instance, religion did indeed produce a context within which he could speak "freely" or as "free" as any slave might during this time. O'Neale points out that "Hammon's discourses were biblically based for both spiritual and civil reasons. Often . . . evangelists used the concepts of 'faith' and 'repentance' as necessary facts of personal soul-searching preceding salvation."[22] Further, Hammon's " 'religious' advice" was used as a means of "directly challenging societal slave laws and the conscience of the church."[23] Phillip Richards goes a step further, arguing convincingly for Hammon's work as having "absorbed the politicized Christian discourse of the war years . . . drawing upon conventions of Protestant rhetoric to promote black uplift."[24] Further, from his exhortations to humility and against drunkenness, rioting, swearing, and other abominations, Hammon "drew upon the jeremiad to exhort his community . . . [to] moral and spiritual regeneration."[25] In light of his appropriation of the millennial language of the Revolution, adoption of "an African patriot persona" in each of his writings to "enlighten minds . . . encourage fellow servants" as well as his adopting of a "nationalism [that] responds to the social experience of blacks"[26] Jupiter Hammon not only demonstrates expert skill in manipulating his knowledge of biblical literacy, but may well be among the earliest in a line of Black reformers in the United States. In this context, Hammon should rightly be repositioned within the canon of early Black nationalists. Further, this view of his "not so subtle" use of religious protest suggests a reconsideration of the categories that are included in Afrocentric poetry, speeches, and literary history. Far from suggesting that Hammon's "Address to the Negroes in the State of New York" be considered a proto–Black nationalist manifesto, his religious productions suggest not only that the spiritual is political, but also that his command of the biblical language and its dual meanings in the eighteenth century provides yet another link for the study of early Black aesthetics and consciousness—a long overdue redemption of this significant early figure.

61

James Albert Gronniosaw's awareness of spiritual liberation was equally perplexing, as the Reverend Walter Shirley reminds the reader in the preface to Gronniosaw's narrative that "he belong'd to the Redeemer of lost Sinners; he was the Purchase of his Cross; and therefore the Lord undertook to bring him by a Way that he knew not" (preface).[27] Sometime later, Gronniosaw himself would admit during a post-conversion moment "for 'I know that my REDEEMER liveth,' and I'm thankful for every trial and trouble that I've met with, as I am not without hope that they have been all sanctified to me."[28] Gronniosaw's experiences suggest that his knowledge of the Bible is extensive. Moreover, his narration of the coincidence and timeliness of the precise words of Scripture that appear to him almost out of heaven, as if God were speaking directly to him, suggests the value of religion for gaining some level of control over his narrative. If, indeed, as William Andrews suggest, "to preface is to prejudice"[29] the outline of scriptural references suggests a way of mapping out the terrain of spiritual removes that provide a parallel if conventional conversion. Notably, while Gronniosaw's relating of his distress at his master's frightening sermons—which confirm John's revelation about Jesus's return to exact judgment on the all the world—initially depicts the enslaved Black man as a helpless victim of both earthly and heavenly masters, the African narrator follows with a scriptural confirmation of God's grace as the "Lamb of God." Gronniosaw thus evokes the agency and power extended to him through Jesus's redemption. Gronniosaw's relating of scriptural proof texts that speak to him, despite the troubling outside world of hypocritical Christians (in Holland and England), slaveholders, thieves, and other undesirables, confirms, comforts, appeases, and guides him during mourning the loss of friends and family. Not unlike for other early Black spiritual autobiographers it is the Word that ultimately provides the structure for his narrative world—for his story. The "footsteps of Providence" thus leading him, guided by the Word and redeemed by a living God, Gronniosaw may indeed be a "stranger in the world, and a pilgrim," but he does not miss the opportunity to remind his reader of his sojourn as a choice without making apology for the evil in this world so drastically different from his life as "the Grandson of a King . . . who, at home [in Bornou and clothed in gold] was . . . guarded by slaves, so that no indifferent person might approach" him.[30] Ultimately, it is a secure grounding in the Scripture that maintains him. Thus, he is secure in his justification as a saint redeemed by the blood of Christ, "waiting patiently for" the Lord's deliverance, he ends his narrative and this prayer with the biblical sign of confirmation, "Amen."[31]

Unlike those of narrators before him, Marrant's narrative of conversion first announces redemption in the voice of a young white convert. Mary Scott's dying plea to "be with my Lord and his redeemed Children in Glory" reminds us both of the little white girl's "tears" that "God would wipe away"[32] and those of the "little negro children" who had been so "savagely flogg'd" that "blood" like tears "ran" from their bodies.[33] Marrant, the black "free Carpenter," gives the Word of God to "the little negro children"[34] and through "a feeling concern for the salvation of [his] countrymen" prays "constantly" for his "brethren, for [his] kinsmen, according to the flesh."[35] Amid the dissonant voices of "strangers . . . Indian tribes . . . black nations . . . [and] vast multitudes, of hard tongues, and . . . strange speech" Marrant conducts a symphony of angels from "the kingdoms of [God's] worlds."[36] Thus, the themes carried forward in the "song of Moses, and of the Lamb" carried particular significance for "Marrant, A Black (Now going to Preach the GOSPEL In Nova-Scotia)."[37] In these biblical verses are echoed Marrant's personal redemption from sin—"The Lord was pleased to set my soul at perfect liberty"—[38]and the communal redemption and deliverance of all people including Marrant's Black brethren and kinsmen. Indeed, Marrant's engagement with the Bible in this rather short narrative provides compelling evidence of the level of depth and extent to which early Black itinerant preachers were immersed in biblical knowledge. If, as Brooks maintains, Marrant "believed himself a prophet, sent to Nova Scotia to initiate the redemption of scattered Africa,"[39] then his attention to the biblical text only served to reinforce such a belief. Consequently, when Marrant "posits blackness, as a marker of chosenness"[40] he uses the language of prophecy to declare that "black people [not only] were on their own timetable and that prophetic activity had not passed away among them" but also were "actors in their own divinely intended history."[41] Significantly, biblical prophecy "was not meant to pacify" Blacks "but rather to embolden them."[42] Rather than assuming "Africa to be the foreordained destination for American blacks," Marrant "particularized the significance of black suffering to the covenant relationship between God and his modern black Israel . . . preach[ing] that God had chosen the enslaved and oppressed descendants of Africa as special witnesses to and emblems of his overruling power." Marrant's ability to extend and reconstruct narratives of empowerment for early Black Christians is testament to his proficiency in the Word. Culturally and spiritually redeemed through such biblical paraphrase, early Black religious writers like Marrant found it unnecessary to reconcile slavery and skin-color prejudice dysfunctionally with Christianity. Instead, they "honored the paradoxes they lived as God's chosen people."[43] Hence, their works demand serious scholarly attention and reconsideration from all regions of the Atlantic.

While Equiano familiarizes us with the conditions under which redemption is both "sought" and "known" in a far less sacred context than the other Black writers, his secular references evince a similar exegetical prowess. Equiano describes redemption in the context of African slavery and the method used to acquire slaves. Notably, if an African chief who has started a war with express intent of capturing and selling "his fellow creatures" into slavery is captured, "it is thought dangerous to let him survive, and no ransom can save him, though all other prisoners may be redeemed."[44] Admittedly, Equiano may indeed have borrowed Willem Bosman's account of the preemptive strike against those Africans who profit from inciting wars and the attendant slave trade. "If the person who occasioned the beginning of the war be taken, they will not easily admit him to ransom . . . for fear he should in future form some new design against their repose."[45] In this passage, the Black narrator further amplifies the dire retributive consequences for African enslavers. That is, his choice of words not only points to them as those who are irreclaimable or irredeemable, but also sheds light on Equiano's fluency with the language of Christian redemption and his ability to manipulate it to political ends.

In the late eighteenth century, three narrators offer accounts of the *most remarkable particulars, wonderful dealings,* and *interesting life* from each man's point of view as an African prince, a Black, and an African, respectively.[46] Such scriptural transformations as prophecy, death, and blood covenants link early Black writers. Thus, while we may see the result of religious doctrines and influence in the nineteenth century, when we look beyond Douglass we see in the literature of the eighteenth-century Black writers the transformation of Calvinism, the restructuring of the Calvinist doctrine of pre-destination, and, moreover, the powerful use made by these early Black writers of their biblical literacy to refit or retool the purposes to which such doctrine may have originally been used. Clearly, early Black writers' selective adoption and adaptation of doctrine suggest their complex and sophisticated level of biblical literacy. One such example is their repeated use of nonannotated Scripture reference in both religious and secular forms. Thus, the power of radical theology would never have been possible without the support of Black writers' biblical literacy. From Genesis to Revelation these authors recover sacred biblical meaning with stellar acumen and alacrity. Importantly, because "authors were trained, ordained, and sophisticated interpreters,"[47] they were able to extend the boundaries of biblical forms while maintaining the integrity and the sacredness of the Word.

65

As such, we do justice to this literature and the worlds such works place forward when we extend the boundaries of secular and sacred canons and celebrate and transgress tradition, convention, gender, genre, race, and class. As we move beyond our limited views of religion, culture, and history, we enliven and reconstitute meaning necessary to re-member Africa, America, and Afro-British America within the context of the antebellum literature—respecting the Word, the Black World, and Black letters.

Notes

1. John Saillant, "Origins of African American Biblical Hermeneutics in Eighteenth-Century Black Opposition," in *African Americans and the Bible: Sacred Texts and Social Textures,* ed. Vincent L. Winbush (New York: Continuum, 2003), 248.

2. Literary scholarship of the past twenty-five years has allowed rigorous exploration of both the depth and the breadth of the eighteenth-century Black writers' use of religious models of protest and cultural self-identification drawn from the Bible. Important historical and critical studies include Vincent Carretta, *Equiano the African: Biography of a Self-Made Man* (Athens: University of Georgia Press, 2005); Joanna Brooks, *American Lazarus: Religion and the Rise of African American and Native American Literatures* (New York: Oxford University Press, 2003); John Saillant, *Black Puritan, Black Republican: The Life and Thought of Lemuel Haynes, 1753-1833* (New York: Oxford University Press, 2003); Katherine Bassard, *Spiritual Interrogations: Culture, Gender, and Community in Early African American Women's Writing* (Princeton: Princeton University Press 1999); David R. Proper,

Lucy Terry Prince: Singer of History (Deerfield: Pocumtuck Valley Memorial Association, 1997); Rafia Zafar, We Wear the Mask: African Americans Write American Literature 1760–1870 (New York: Columbia University Press, 1997); Sondra O'Neale, Jupiter Hammon and the Biblical Beginnings of African-American Literature (Metuchen: Scarecrow Press, 1993); Angelo Costanzo, Surprising Narrative: Olaudah Equiano and the Beginnings of Black Autobiography (New York: Greenwood Press, 1987).

3. I make use of the oft-cited censure of Wheatley's poetry by Thomas Jefferson in Notes on the State of Virginia—"Religion indeed has produced a Phyllis [sic] Whately [sic] but it could not produce a poet. The compositions published under her name are below the dignity of criticism"—in order to signify on the continuum of criticism that has radicalized, apologized, or patronized the religious aspects of the works of early Black literary writers. Henry Louis Gates Jr. puts it best (in his 2002 lecture "Mister Jefferson and The Trials of Phillis Wheatley") when he maintains, "It's striking that Jefferson and Amiri Baraka, two figures in American letters who would agree on little else, could agree on the terms of their indictment of Phillis Wheatley." From less harshly critical and somewhat benign eighteenth-century reviewers to post-1960s detractors, post-1980s apologists, and post-1990s Afrocentric revisionists, religion has often operated as somewhat of a straw man or foil to depoliticize and deaestheticize early black writing.

4. Patricia Liggins Hill's Call and Response: The Riverside Anthology of the African Literary Tradition (Boston: Houghton Mifflin, 2003) is an exception as one of the few if not the only collection that gives serious attention rather than mere coverage to (pre-1900) Black literature and historical contexts.

5. I applaud the tremendous contributions of Riverside, Bedford, and Norton anthologies of African American literature to the study of Black literature in the United States. However, such considerable achievements represent only a fraction of the work that needs to be done before African American literary studies can even begin to approach the depth and breadth of the comprehensive ranges (demographic, historical, and cultural) of Anglo-American and European literary studies. A conspicuous example is the expectation that a single anthology bear the burden of in-depth coverage of a literary tradition—from Hammon's "An Evening Thought on Salvation" to Lauryn Hill's "Final Hour"—that is nearly two hundred and fifty years old (1760–2007) spanning three continents (Africa, Europe, and North America) with persistently emerging genres, works, and cultures.

6. I refer here to a kind of synthesis including but not limited to William Andrews Sisters of the Spirit: Three Black Women's Autobiographies of the Nineteenth Century (Bloomington, Indiana University Press, 1986); Adam Potkay and Sandra Burr, Black Atlantic Writers of the 18th Century: Living the New Exodus in England and the Americas (New York: St. Martins Press, 1995), and Carretta's Unchained Voices: An Anthology of Black Authors in the English-Speaking World of the 18th Century (Lexington: University Press of Kentucky, 1996) and Equiano's unabridged Interesting Narrative (New York: Penguin, 2003).

7. Gen. 20:22. King James Version (KJV).

8. Acts 17:24 (KJV).

9. Col. 1:14 (KJV).

10. Col. 1:13 (KJV).

11. Phillis Wheatley, "On Being Brought," in The Collected Works of Phillis Wheatley, ed. John C. Shields (New York: Oxford University Press, 1988), 18, line 4.

12. Wheatley, "On the Death of . . . Whitefield," 22, line 36.

13. Julian D. Mason, "Introduction," in The Poems of Phillis Wheatley, Revised and Enlarged Edition with an Additional Poem (Chapel Hill: University of North Carolina Press, 1989), 4.

14. Ibid., 15.

15. Ibid., 14.

16. William J. Scheick, "Subjection and Prophecy in Phillis Wheatley's Verse Paraphrases of Scripture," *College Literature* 22, no. 3 (October 1995): 122.

17. Matt. 27:61.

18. Wheatley, "Phillis's Reply to the Answer," 144, line 22.

19. Jupiter Hammon, "An Address to Miss Wheatley," in *America's First Negro Poet: The Complete Works of Jupiter Hammon of Long Island*, ed. Stanley Austin Ransom Jr. (Port Washington: Kennikat Press, 1970), 49, line 64.

20. Sondra O'Neale, *Jupiter Hammon and the Biblical Beginnings of African-American Literature* (Metuchen, NJ: Scarecrow Press, 1993), 45.

21. Hammon, "An Address," 112. My emphases on "youth" and "young" are intended to point to Hammon's obvious inclusion of Wheatley among those "young Negroes" who should be physically free. At the same time his description of her as "pious" obviously claims her as worthy of a similar freedom in the spiritual realm.

22. O'Neale, *Jupiter Hammon*, 88.

23. Ibid., 89.

24. Phillip M. Richards, "Nationalist Themes in the Preaching of Jupiter Hammon," *Early American Literature* 25, no. 2, (September 1990): 124.

25. Ibid., 126–127.

26. Ibid., 127.

27. James Albert Gronniosaw, *A Narrative of the Most Remarkable Particulars in the Life of James Albert Ukawsaw Gronniosaw, An African Prince, As Related By Himself*, in *Unchained Voices: An Anthology of Black Authors in the English-Speaking World of the 18th Century*, ed. Vincent Carretta (Lexington: University Press of Kentucky, 1996), 33.

28. Ibid., 48.

29. William Andrews, *To Tell a Free Story: The First Century of Afro-American Autobiography*, 1760–1865 (Urbana: University of Illinois Press, 1988), 35.

30. Gronniosaw, *Narrative*, 48.

31. Ibid., 53.

32. John Marrant, *A Narrative of the Lord's Wonderful Dealings With John Marrant, a Black (Now Going to Preach the Gospel in Nova-Scotia) Born in New York, in North-America*, in *Unchained Voices: Anthology of Black Authors in the English-Speaking World of the 18th Century*, ed. Vincent Carretta (Lexington: University Press of Kentucky, 1996), 125.

33. Ibid., 123.

34. Ibid., 123.

35. Ibid., 126.

36. Ibid., 127.

37. Ibid., 110.

38. Ibid., 114.

39. Joanna Brooks, *American Lazarus: Religion and the Rise of African American and Native American Literatures* (New York: Oxford University Press, 2003), 87.

40. Ibid., 94.

41. Ibid., 95.

42. Ibid., 108.

43. Ibid. One way of honoring such paradoxes was to understand that "oppression was not the consequence of insufficient efforts but rather the evidence of their covenant with God" (ibid., 104–5).

44. Olaudah Equiano, The *Interesting Narrative of the Life of Olaudah Equiano, or Gustavus Vassa, The African, Written By Himself. Ninth Edition, 1794,* in *Olaudah Equiano: The Interesting Narrative and Other Writings,* ed. Vincent Carretta (New York: Penguin, 2003), 39.

45. Ibid., 244n 63.

46. Emphasis here is intended to underscore the similar African significatory practices as evinced in the title of their respective spiritual autobiographical works—James Albert Ukawsaw Gronniosaw's A *Narrative of the Most Remarkable Particulars in the Life of James Albert Ukawsaw Gronniosaw, An African Prince;* John Marrant's A *Narrative of the Lord's Wonderful Dealings With John Marrant, a Black;* and Olaudah Equiano's The *Interesting Narrative of the Life of Olaudah Equiano, or Gustavus Vassa, the African*—most notably, their signaling of their Christian identification in the words of the religious fervor of the Great Awakening (remarkable, wonderful, interesting) and their identification of the respective markers racial and cultural identities (African prince, a Black, the African), both common narrative conventions during this historical period, which coincidentally worked to establish the spiritual and secular realms of their words and worlds.

47. Brooks, *American Lazerus,* 17.

Phillip M. Richards

*A*nglo-American Continuities of Civic and Religious Thought in the Institutional World of Early Black Writing

EARLY AFRICAN-AMERICAN WRITERS SUCH AS JOHN JEA, GEORGE White, and David Walker explicitly addressed the task of African-American social formation in the postrevolutionary and early national periods. Creating voluntary organizations, exhorting their fellows to citizenship, and promoting education, Black leaders and their followers often drew the anger and contempt of whites. Afro-Americans attempting to exercise political autonomy inevitably confronted the limits placed by white American society upon their existence as citizens.[1] This conflict led early Black writers to an understanding of the consequences of political exclusion and civic estrangement. Predictably this understanding drew upon the ideological resources of the new nation. In the midst of this appropriation, the early Puritan Protestantism underlying Black political life was secularized into a romantic-evangelical worldview. This romantic-evangelical worldview gave secular sophistication to Black understanding of political and social alienation as well as of "interest." Whatever its essentially Anglo-American nature, this admixture of evangelical piety, romantic impulses, and revolutionary rhetoric pushed Black writers into an ethnically centered nationalism. The continuing American Revolution anticipated by Thomas Jefferson emerged full-born in early nineteenth-century Black radicalism.

Nearly all of the New England and Mid-Atlantic states took up some form of emancipation after the Revolutionary War. As a result many Blacks settled in urban areas. The work of Richard Allen, Absalom Jones, John Marrant, George White, William Whipper, and David Walker exemplifies a growing early nineteenth-century Black confrontation with the trauma accompanying Black community formation: the newly established African-American churches, voluntary associations, benevolent groups, fraternal orders, missionary societies, and educational organizations.[2] As the speeches of Black institutional leaders show, these early groups conceived of themselves as organic social communities centered on traditional Protestant social piety. For early Black writers, this piety served as an active principle by which African-American Christians enacted communal love. Speaking of such charity, Prince Saunders observed in the late eighteenth century:

> Such, and sublimely excellent, are the fruits of a spirit of Christian Charity and practical beneficence; for to it alone the glory is due of having placed the weak under the protection of their stronger brethren; for she unceasingly labours to improve all the varying circumstances and conditions of mankind: so that, among those who profess her true spirit, the love of our neighbour is not an inactive principle, but it is real beneficence, and they, like the good Samaritan in the gospel, evince their sincerity by ministering to the necessities, and in labouring for the welfare, improvement and happiness of mankind.[3]

First conceptualized in earlier Puritan writings such as John Winthrop's "Model of Christian Charity," benevolence made practical demands upon its Black constituents. In particular, it required regular financial contributions. A trusted and respected member of the community, a treasurer, frequently husbanded these monies. In case of a member's death, the widow and her family received funds to support themselves and to place the children in an honest living. Through these procedures, Christian benevolence sustained Black social structures supporting communal order and providing for its persistence.[4]

The new Black communities also promoted social order through the education and socialization of youth. The instruction of African-American children often depended upon the existence of education

societies that raised money for schools, hired teachers, and ran the institutions. African-American activists provided encouragement as well as
more tangible resources. Black leaders such as William Hamilton frequently exhorted the youth to cultivate the arts and sciences. This cultivation extended to formal learning, which issued in a mastery of the
surrounding world.[5] As they inculcated children in this mastery, Afro-
American intellectuals envisioned themselves perpetuating their community's benevolent social order, instilling secular rationalism, and
preparing the African American society's future leaders.

The notion of mastery appears vividly in central texts in early nineteenth-century Black writing. Black orators such as William Hamilton and
William Whipper linked the notion of intellectual and voluntary capacity
with an Enlightenment view of a world created by a reasonable God, run
by rational laws, and divinely placed under the government of intelligent
men. Education's function lay in its promotion of perception and reason,
the cultivation of the mind—and a rationally organized worldview. The
end of such a rationally organized worldview was purposive action.

71

> The acquisition of knowledge is not the only design of a liberal education;
> its primary design is to discipline the mind itself to strengthen and enlarge
> its powers, to form habits of close and accurate thinking, and to acquire a
> facility of classifying and arranging, analyzing and comparing our ideas on
> different subjects. Without this preparatory exercise, our ideas will be
> superficial and obscure, and all the knowledge we acquire will be but a
> confused mass thrown together without arrangement and incapable of
> useful application.[6]

In the language of the early orators *useful application* referred to the world
of the professions and acceptable moneymaking ventures. These Black
orators were the intellectual counterparts of early African-American
entrepreneurs such as James Forten and Paul Cuffe, who entered the
world of business and thus faced a world dominated by capitalist economic organization. *Usefulness,* in the discourse of both Whipper and
Hamilton, represented an African-American accommodation to a secularized, economically rational world.

Cultivating spiritual as well as secular education, these writers
propounded a middle-class Protestant worldview that was sacred and

worldly. This outlook took the form of both a middle-class Protestantism and a rationalist perspective reflected throughout early African-American writing. In this view, the success of Black American life depended upon the existence of families that maintained social order, socialized children, and reproduced a middle-class world for future generations. These values are apparent in a 1796 letter written by the African Humane Society at Philadelphia to the African Union Society in Newport.

> Secondly, we advise such as you as have not been taught reading, writing, and the first principles of arithmetic, to acquire them as early as possible. Carefully attend to the instruction of your children in the same simple and useful branches of education. Cause them likewise early and frequently to read the holy scriptures; they contain among other discoveries the precious record of the "Original Equality" of the [need] for universal justice and benevolence, which are derived from the relation of the human race to each other in a common father.[7]

Practical success, ethical behavior, and political self-consciousness combined into a coherent point of view. However, these converging religious and secular aims produced a volatile ideological combination. Fueled by middle-class rationality, Black writers quickly pointed out that educated youths faced little prospect of work and that racist politics overlooked the contradictions of a segregated democracy. This new consciousness propelled the radicalization of African-American communities in the late eighteenth century and the early antebellum period.

The most visible sign of radicalization occurred when the Black intellectuals considered the dislocated African-American majority surrounding them. Proponents of Black uplift looking at the Black masses through the lens of middle-class Protestantism inevitably responded to the plight of the Black masses around them. Such writers highlighted the disabling consequences of life outside stable families, mutual aid societies, and churches. Assuming the larger African-American community to be dysfunctional and their wills misdirected, early Black writers often referred to masses as *wretched*, a term that would become an important metaphor in David Walker's writing. This opposition between the estranged cultivated speaker and the "wretched" masses appears in a fast day statement written by individuals in a Black benevolent society in Newport. The document's desperate tone suggests the literate authors' political concern for the state of less fortunate Blacks.

> We, taking into consideration the calamitous state into which we are brought by the righteous hand of God, being strangers & outcasts in a strange land, attended with many disadvantages and evils, with respect to living, which are like to continue on us and and on our children, while we and they live in this country, and the yet more wretched state of many hundreds of thousands of our brethren, who are in the most abject state of many hundreds of our brethren, who are in the most abject slavery, in the West Indies, and in the American States, many of whom are treated in the most inhumane and cruel manner, and are sunk down in ignorance, stupidity, and vice, and considering the unhappy circumstances of our brethren, the nature of our brethren, the nations of Africa, from whom we sprang, being in heathenish darkness, & barbarity, and are, and have been for so many years.[8]

In the eyes of Protestant Black observers, slavery destroyed those social structures and worldviews that would otherwise order the lives of the Black masses. In documents such as this, the African-American elite become spokesmen for an underclass that cannot organize, understand, or speak for itself.

As early Black American writers considered the debilitating affects of racism, they inevitably encountered their own alienation from full participation in American social and civic life. Seeking membership in professions, early Black intellectuals were forced to face their own marginal status vis-à-vis those institutions that underwrote leadership in the new nation. The writings of these figures show their attention to the "inner psychological life" that transpired as they sought to enter leadership positions. For them to become pastors, their era's career open to Black talent, was to find themselves hamstrung by institutionalized requirements for the ministry, the antagonism of the white masses, and the insecure life of itinerant ministers. To undertake professional life was to confront the forces pushing them away from civic participation. This confrontation could only deepen their estrangement from the fulfillments offered by the new American society.

The vocational, social, and political anxieties faced by aspiring Black ministers parallel those experienced by late eighteenth- and early nineteenth-century white American writers such as Charles Brockden Brown, Washington Irving, and William Cullen Bryant. A modernized American society unmediated by multigenerational cultural traditions surrounded white intellectuals with a fluid and unstable atmosphere. This instability registered itself in the difficulty experienced by young intellectuals making the life-settling choices of career, mate, and social or political orientation. These white writers often found themselves describing the dilemmas of their era's youth within their literary works. William Cullen Bryant depicts the tensions of this world in verse such as "To a Waterfowl," "Thanatopsis," and "To Cole, the Painter, Departing for Europe": all of them works of a writer confronting an increasingly secularized world without visible supports for the anxieties of early adulthood.[9] Similarly, Cooper's *The Pioneers* and *The Pathfinder* not only present styles of manhood appropriate for the settlement of the frontier, but also pose these styles as alternatives for young white men preparing for the responsibilities of adulthood. The image of the young New Englander seeking not only wealth but political influence appears— however comically—in Washington Irving's depiction of Ichabod Crane, the mock-hero of "The Legend of Sleepy Hollow." Young white men represented by Cooper, Franklin, and Bryant lean upon a self-reliance grounded upon intellectual prowess, a romantic vision of nature, or world-mastering skill shaped through survival in the frontier. The world responds to their exertions of will with material reward, desirable women, and significant places in the social order. Ambitious young Black men entered the evangelical ministry relying upon charismatic authority, organizational skill, and the support of transatlantic evangelicals to achieve careers that grounded them in American society. The narratives of George White and John Jea depict the careers of ambitious young Black men following the only profession open to African-Americans of talent, that of the minister.[10] Whites and Jea's memoirs depict such youthful Black ministers negotiating opportunity and obstacles as they enter pastoral careers where they may achieve social power. These ministers typically center their narratives around the acquisition of professional literacy, institution building, and literary expression. As they undertake these enterprises, White and Jea appropriate the political dimension of evangelical discourse and run with it. They depict their ministerial and ecclesiastical efforts as forms of political organization, often but not always carried out among Black people. In the process, these pastors confront an increasingly institutionalized and often anti-Black world of late eighteenth- and early nineteenth-century America. Although Jea and White finally enter British society, their evangelical importance has been fueled by a struggle for power within the formal associations of American church life. Through their charisma, prophetic leadership, and wish-fulfilling self-invention, these ministers acquire a political and social status otherwise denied to Blacks. Unable to enter an increasingly modern society on its own terms, these writers fashioned an authoritative persona based on an appeal to "otherworldly" realities.

Significantly, White and Jea's depiction of their self-creation echoes the depiction of successful evangelical careers in the lives of late eighteenth-century Black southerners who entered the ministry after conversion and often found success beyond American borders. These included George Leile and David George in Virginia as well as Boston King in South Carolina. They experienced conversion at the hands of revivalists and commitment to an itinerant ministry. Both David George and Boston King would found churches in Canada and later in Sierra Leone. Leile would start a church in Kingston, Jamaica. Variously encountering hostility to their itinerancy, capture into slavery, and racist opposition to their churches these figures, in their lives anticipated the narrative structures of White and Jea.[11]

These experiences of these earlier figures share with the White and Jea narratives elements that the later ministers would work into a more complex tale of providential direction and design. Later narratives will more pointedly echo the experience of not only Jesus but also the New Testament apostles, ministerial leadership, and authority as they depict the aspiring minister maintaining and institutionalizing his charisma as a revivalist, settled preacher, and a literary voice in the text. Seen against the backdrop of the earlier narrators, White and Jea reveal a newly minted insight into the possibilities of a highly reactive Protestant theology. They seem to grasp instinctively the power of Protestant piety to define plausible social roles and to endow them with a legitimacy accepted throughout American society. This reactive potential played an important part in the radicalizing force of Protestant Christianity for Blacks.

One early eighteenth-century writer who begins to grasp the full narrative possibilities of Protestant piety is John Marrant, whose narrative was written in the 1780s. This autobiographical narrative shows a young Black man choosing the charismatic style of a prophetic ministry amid the tensions of the post–Revolutionary War era.[12] Marrant's narrative tells the story of a young man converted by Whitefield from a life of carousing to piety. The newly pious Marrant discovers his vocation as a minister and enters life as an itinerant preacher. In the narrative's central episode he is captured by Indians, whom he eventually converts, incidentally saving his life. In the course of this experience Marrant has wholly assumed the charismatic, prophetic model exemplified by Whitefield, who has spiritually awakened him in a single encounter. Drawing upon this style, Marrant eventually finds a rousing reception as a revival preacher in England.

Marrant's narrative is a story of professional vocation and success. As a literary structure, it appropriates spiritual autobiography and the captivity narrative in order to define the autobiographical subject's legitimacy in charismatic terms. As a preacher, Marrant will rely not only on formal learning but on religious experience and prophetic demeanor. George Whitefield who converts him—a thoughtless young musician concerned only with amusement—is Marrant's exemplary preacher: a dramatic, soul-piercing evangelist who in a moment's encounter can decisively awaken the sinner. Marrant becomes such a preacher in the course of the narrative. As he does so, the story moves from a realistic account of his early life, youthful musicianship, and conversion to a dreamlike romance account of his life, wandering in the woods where Native Americans capture him.

Marrant's achievement of charisma emerges when his eventual success as a revivalist fulfills—again in a dreamlike way—the young man's earlier desires. Marrant, who earlier lived only for physical pleasure, now experiences deep gratification in the woods eating "sweet grass" and drinking "muddy water." Saving his life through the conversion of a Native American, Marrant enacts a significant repetition of his earlier deeply affecting transformation at the hands of George Whitefield. Interestingly, the young Marrant's implicit desire to wield an emotional and psychological impact upon his audience through music finds expression in his successful revivalist preacher, even as George Whitefield's skill anticipated his preaching.

Marrant's captivity sequence is a wish-fulfilling fantasy in which the narrator not only imagines his psychological, intellectual, and professional fulfillment, but also provides autobiographical "evidence" of his prophetic status. In the woods, the young erstwhile carousing Marrant becomes an authentic prophet, an identity that his enthusiastic reception in England underlines. Indeed both prophecy and prophetic confirmation in England well represent a stature that he, like George, Liele, and Boston King, can only find in Jamaica or England and Sierra Leone, as opposed to the United States. Marrant's charismatic style represents the way in which a barely learned ambitious young man may exercise intellectual, spiritual, and political authority in the world.

Marrant illustrates the psychological dynamics by which charisma is achieved and exercised. However, his narrative is narrowly focused when considered as autobiography. More importantly, his experience reveals a radicalizing energy. In the woods amid the Indians he imagines a prophetic stature that he later realizes in his own ministry. With noticeable literary skill, Marrant depicts himself as a self-made prophet who literally wills himself into being. To be sure, he has little to tell us of his family life, his social life with people surrounding him, and his own psychological and intellectual development. Not only does he lack Sancho's and Equiano's literary tools that would equip him for such a task, but Marrant clearly conceives of his life in much more limited terms. His charismatic posture—for all of its revivalist power—represents a relatively narrow personal and political fulfillment grounded primarily in institutional achievement. However, this achievement represents the fulfillment of the earliest aspirations of a onetime popular musician who from the beginning enjoyed wielding influence over a crowd.

The early nineteenth-century narratives by George White and John Jea depict the attempts of later, but similarly disadvantaged Black ministers to assert themselves professionally and institutionally. Within these narratives, however, the authors make an even more forceful statement of the oppositional stance of Black professional and institutional life to the mainstream of Black culture. George White, raised by a relatively tolerant white master, as was Marrant, also experiences conversion and enters the ministry. However, he links both manumission and religious experience with freedom, saying that after gaining temporal freedom he attempted to achieve spiritual freedom. This reference to the two freedoms begins a central conflict within the book, the tension between his desire to carry out a charismatic evangelical ministry and the formal requirements of an increasingly professionalized ministry.

The chief conflict in White's narrative takes place between his charismatic powers that win revival converts and the restraints of white ministerial associations who for a long time refuse to license White. After successive attempts to gain a license, White gains the association's approval and a license, which is renewed. This too implies the existence of an "inner life" of the aspiring leader. White's clear intent to legitimize himself as a pastor leads him largely to ignore the implications of a ministerial life spent traveling from revival to revival apart from one's family. How does the aspiring pastor bear this separation? When White does take up his response to the plight of a dying sister, the autobiographical narrative emphasizes—not the complexities and probable discouragements of mourning—but rather the woman's deathbed conversion and the minister's funeral sermon with which the work closes.

White's sermon narrative–ending elegy represents a professional mastery of his Black civic world and closure to his quest for institutional standing. This mastery not only embodies the official social recognition of the ministerial license but also a mastery over the crisis of a beloved one's death. The sermon represents White's acquired skill in addressing and resolving the traumas faced by his community—in a form that not only gives solace but also transforms dislocation into moral instruction. The sermon sets forth the establishment of social order; however, as the story shows, this order-establishing capacity has been gained only at the cost of conflict with the larger society.

In many ways John Jea's narrative is a culmination of many of the tendencies described in Marrant and White. Jea's narrative defines even more forcefully than White's the tension between the institutionalization of Black religious life and the growing early nineteenth-century

78

restraints on organized African-American activity. Jea pointedly links his temporal bondage as a slave with his spiritual bondage as a sinner. And he sees his conversion as both a literal and a metaphorical manumission. After his conversion, a court rules him a free man by virtue of his identity as a Christian.

Having been converted, Jea begins his activities as an itinerant minister, learning to the read the Bible and therefore educating himself. After a successful period of preaching in New York, he gathers a congregation and with the help of white patrons establishes a church. His success as a pastor leads to more itinerant preaching abroad, and eventually he begins to preach in Boston and finally in England and Europe. He depicts his life as a traveling preacher in terms modeled not only upon Awakening itinerants but also upon the Jesus of the Gospels and the apostles of Acts. In the midst of these journeys he is reduced at times to labor as a slave, a sailor, and a cook among other tasks. Like Jesus, he is at least once confronted over his theological beliefs: his adherence to Calvinist doctrine of predestination and its consistency with the evangelical command for voluntary repentance.

Jea's extended account of his journeys finds coherence in the book's two thematically defined sections. The first, his entrance into the ministry, focuses around his conversion-liberation, choice of vocation, and establishment of a pastorate. The book's second section focuses upon his extended apostlelike missions abroad. The thematic development of both sections turns upon the conflict between Jea's commitment to his spiritual goal and the challenges offered by the world to the fulfillment of his aspirations as a saint and a minister. In particular, Jea's apostle work creates an alternate series of experiences: affirmations and implicitly worldly denials of Jea's authenticity as a prophet. Taken as a whole these conflicts resolve into a statement of the memoir's theme: God's sustained affirmation of Jea's prophetic identity and enterprise.

More than any of the other American-centered Black autobiographers, Jea takes account of the process by which his persona-subject acquires a social and historical perspective on his experience and its workings. Equiano's literary achievement emerges from his success in depicting his persona's growing consciousness of himself and the world around him. On a somewhat cruder level, Jea is under way on a similar narrative enterprise. Jea's narrator seeks a spiritual understanding of the world and his place in it. However, he grounds this understanding in naïve empirical terms. As a youth, Jea acquires a negative idea of Christianity from the actual behavior of Christians only to learn after his conversion how to read a providential design in his day-to-day life.

In this narrative the divine glory and providential design represent a counterweight to the earthly forces of local antagonism, racism, and ecclesiastical politics, all of which threaten Jea's aspirations. His "spiritual" understanding of the world allows him to face those events, which on their face appear to deny the reality of his prophetic mission and identity. Seen in this perspective Jea's spiritual understanding borders upon what in David Walker will become a racial consciousness, capable of placing Black historical and institutional experience in a New Light. Future Black writers will draw upon Jea's use of the evangelical motif of spiritual awakening in order to exhort their African-American audiences to this new consciousness.

In an incisive article treating Jea and his ministry, John Saillant argues that Jea misunderstood the actual extent of his "freedom," the degree to which he participated in the political equality devolved upon him in postrevolutionary America. Saillant correctly points to Jea's periodic reduction to the status of slave and laborer as a sign of the tenuousness of Jea's social position in the post–Revolutionary War world.[13] Further generalizing Saillant's insight, one might say that Black institution building forced these figures to contemplate the extent to which they participated in white and Black society. Whatever their answer to this dilemma, they implicitly faced the quasi-ideological task of providing plausibility for struggling Black institutions that frequently faced white attacks.

As early Black authors considered secular alienation and estrangement in religious terms they inevitably came upon protoromantic interpretations of their contemporary African-American condition. The appropriation of Protestant ideology to autobiography, moreover, created cultivated narrators who recognized Black instances of alienation and estrangement usually linked to early romantic thought. As does the narrator and autobiographical subject of Olaudah Equiano's memoir, African-American narrators continually narrated the thwarted spiritual mastery of their worlds. In this sense Protestantism sensitizes Black narrators to the phenomenon of alienation as it is described by early Anglo-European romantics. It is not surprising that the distinctive discourse of African Americanization followed the prototypes of Protestant and romantic patterns of alienation that appeared in the writing of nineteenth-century Continental, British, and American figures such as the young Marx of the 1844 *Economic and Philosophical Manuscripts,* the Wordsworth of the 1805 "Preface" to the *Lyrical Ballads,* and the young Emerson of "Man the Reformer." The concept of alienation, which gained widespread currency among nineteenth-century intellectuals, received a highly suggestive statement in the treatment in the writings of the young Marx. For Marx, in his Hegelian phase, alienation in capitalist society consisted of the objectification of the human subject through his estrangement from the product of his labor. The process of estrangement marked the human subject's loss of mastery over his material object, and his entrance into a world of objects governed by purely material forces. The giving of primary value to the object of labor in the marketplace effectively objectified the worker himself. At the heart of the worker's transformation into an object was the dehumanization of labor's role. The assembly line and mechanized workplace could not be sites for human fulfillment. Consequently the worker or human subject instead of appropriating the world for himself becomes an object dominated in a world of other objects and by the material forces of that world.

81

The Black minister-writers initiated a tradition in which African-American intellectuals recognize a similar objectification in their own experience, an alienating process stemming from a dehumanizing estrangement from civic and social life. These minister-writers seek to overcome this alienation from civic life through the assumption of prophetic stances in the revivalist evangelical movements. At the end of their narratives, these writers acquire a self-consciousness that in its own way reflected the dehumanization of the masses that lacked familial, communal, and educational structure. From their Protestant perspective Black writers could imagine a Black dehumanization in this fluid world without structured personal and organizational relations. And increasingly, writers such as David Walker, clearly attuned to the phenomenon of estrangement, reworked an earlier conventional understanding of "wretchedness" to define a Black condition requiring a secular redemption. Walker's insight—whether directly transmitted or not—underlay the narrative posture of Frederick Douglass. In the 1845 *Narrative,* the former slave described his achievement of human fullness as a victory over the estranging dehumanization of slavery. Although Protestantism rejected the notion of a secularized autonomous subjectivity envisioned by Hegel and the young Marx, these early Black writers' awareness of alienation represented a version of secular romantic redemption. And ultimately this insight linked these writers with other exponents of secular redemption such as the young Marx of the 1848 *Philosophical and Economic Manuscripts,* the Emerson of "Man the Reformer," and the Thoreau of *Walden's* first chapter.

In these early Black writers a Calvinist-inflected Protestantism evolves in the African-American experience into an African-American natural supernaturalism. A homemade evangelical romanticism emerges among early Black writers who both seek civic inclusion and decry wretchedness among the masses. This evangelical romanticism implicitly became an ethnically centered nationalism that well may have found a symbolic focus in Americanized versions of African celebrations such as the "ring shout." As the early Black leaders of the free African-American communities did, the Black ministers conceived of an organic Afro-American society, consolidated by benevolence or political interest. The protoromantic evangelism of these writers represented spiritual revival as a means of overcoming wretchedness and reinstating a community of benevolence and shared interest. This romantic nationalism became a secular redemptive means of overcoming the alienation bred of Black exclusion from white American voluntary associations and political entities. The leaders' ability to assert the human fullness of their listeners underwrote their prophetic authority in both Black and white society.

David Walker's complaints about the absence of African-Americans in political life clearly represent not only the plight of his race but personal frustration. As had the Black evangelicals who preceded him, David Walker overcomes his own alienation from civic life by assuming a prophetic role before "wretched" masses that are also estranged. He does so by explicitly building a revivalist stance based on an earlier

Black worldview that centered Christian social order in a citizen's piety and civic virtue. Walker's use of this formulation is predictable given his probable association with revivalists in South Carolina and his certain association with Black political organizations in Boston. In the course of the *Appeal,* Walker articulates this prophetic revivalism in a jeremiad that criticizes the early Black communities for failures in black schooling, preservation of domestic order, maintenance of group unity, and promotion of uplift—all areas of crucial concern to the first African-American free societies. The jeremiad also defines Walker's attack on the consequences of slavery and white racism for America. Within the context of these prophetic sermons, white America faces punishment, an apocalyptic destruction accelerated by racism, slavery, and white oppression.

As does the Emerson of "Self Reliance" or the Thoreau of *Walden's* first chapter, Walker engages in a romantic appropriation of Puritan "awakening" of the conversion process in order to prod his Black audience in particular into political self-consciousness. This self-consciousness is grounded on the critique of American and African-American   society implicit in the romantic evangelical worldview. He shows that the political, religious, and cultural dynamics of early American society has systematically preserved New World wretchedness.[14] That is, Walker argues that Black estrangement stems from the alienating failure to master American society for the fulfillment of oneself and one's people as citizens. Americans have never allowed Blacks the kind of political power that the pharaoh gave to the Israelite Joseph or the entrance into the pharaoh's family that Joseph gained through marriage to the pharaoh's daughter. In this connection, exhortations to acculturation point to the entrapment of Blacks in wretchedness.

One commentator has noted the resemblance of Walker's *Appeal* to the United States Constitution.[15] I would argue that *The Appeal* provokes Black self-consciousness by identifying African-Americans with the outlook implicit in "wretchedness," a worldview that undermines Black humanity. As he accounts for that worldview, Walker attempts "to awaken in the breasts of my afflicted, degraded and slumbering brethren, a spirit of inquiry and investigation respecting our miseries and wretchedness in this Republican Land of Liberty!!!!!!!!!!!!"[16]

As Thomas Paine does in *Common Sense,* Walker reinterprets conventional historical and cultural understandings in order to show that the worldviews imposed by oppressive powers are not inevitable. He intends to shock his Black audience into a new, morally illuminating historical backdrop against which wretchedness might be understood.

> They [proslavery American whites] tell us of the Israelites in Egypt, the Helots in Sparta, and of the Roman Slaves, which last were made up from almost every nation under heaven, whose suffering under those ancient and heathen nations, were, in comparison with ours, under this enlightened and Christian nation, no more than a cipher—or, in other words, those heathen nations of antiquity, had but little more among them than the name and form of slavery; while wretchedness and endless miseries were reserved, apparently in a phial, to be poured out upon our fathers, ourselves and our children.[17]

In this new historical vision, present-day Black suffering appears far more severe than that of the Israelites, the Helots, and Roman slaves. And the oppression of African-Americans in the early nineteenth century becomes an apocalyptic, world-ending suffering: "a phial, to be poured out upon our fathers." Within the context of this exceptional disaster all normal human relations have collapsed. Wretchedness has become the source of the breakdown of civic virtue among the Black masses themselves. At the core of this political submission to tyranny that Walker sees as a massive Black disorganization is the breakdown of domestic life that proceeds from the dehumanizing effects of slavery. "My observer may see fathers beating their sons, mothers their daughters and children their parents, all to pacify the passions of unrelenting tyrants. He may also, see them telling news and lies, making mischief upon one another. These are some of the productions of ignorance, which he will see practiced among my dear brethren who are held in unjust slavery and wretchedness, by avaricious and unmerciful tyrants."[18] At the core of this apparent breakdown is the psychologically corrosive function of an unjust slavery, the practices of avaricious and unmerciful tyrants. Virtue is lacking among Blacks not because they are inherently evil but because they live in a social world that directly attacks their capacity for virtue. As destructive as this Black dislocation are the social frameworks and social knowledge by which wretchedness is preserved.

As an example of such social knowledge, Walker cites *Notes on the State of Virginia* for its pseudoscientific support of the social structures that promote African-American social collapse. At the heart of his attack on Jefferson is Walker's notion that the Virginian writer has made Black social dislocation into a fact of nature rather than a social phenomenon:

> It is not their condition then, but nature, which has produced the distinction. See this, my brethren!! Do you believe that this assertion is swallowed by millions of whites See his writings for the world, and public labors for the United States of America. Do you believe that the assertions of such a man will pass away into oblivion unobserved by this people and the world? If you do you are much mistaken—See how the American people treat us—have we souls in our bodies? I know that there are many swell bellied fellows among us, whose greatest object is to fill their stomachs. Such I do not mean—I am after those who know and feel, that we are MEN, as well as other people.[19]

According to Walker, Jefferson has posited a pseudoscientific racism: the culture's understanding of Black inferiority as part of day-to-day social reality. And the intent of Walker's pamphlet is to rob Jefferson's racism of its socially taken-for-granted status.

Walker also attacks Christianity as another means of legitimizing those supports on which wretchedness is grounded. Through this abuse of Christianity, not only are Blacks degraded below their rightful social station but whites are exalted above their proper place. In this way, the social knowledge of Christianity expounds a radical dislocation of the proper hierarchy within God's world. Those who support human bondage through theology are therefore providing one more ideological sanction for oppression—helping to sustain an ungodly and a wretched human enterprise. Walker goes on to argue that the colonization movement serves a similar legitimizing function. The deepest fear of the opponents of colonization, Walker argues, is that the presence of free blacks will inspire African-Americans who remain in bondage. With this assumption, he asserts that the promotion of the colonization movement could only continue to legitimize the institution of slavery in the United States.

The social consciousness that derives from his observations is intended by Walker to be the basis of a militant Black opposition to the then presently constituted American society. And this opposition would ground itself in a critical understanding of the texts, political movements, and religious institutions that sustain Black wretchedness. In an important sense, Walker advocates a political and social "literacy" that will, as does Jea's "spiritual understanding," allow African-Americans to interpret the world around them in their own interests. Walker evokes this consciousness as an evangelist evokes a consciousness of sin in order to awaken his audience to a transformation. This personal transformation will ultimately be the source of both Black revolt and the construction of an eventual millennial society in which Blacks and whites live together in terms of equality. This evangelical intent appears within Walker's analysis of the intellectual and social structures sustaining wretchedness.

Walker's interest in self-consciousness takes him to a political concept that he identifies more through practical experience than theory. This is a concept of interest in terms of human psychology. Walker's implicitly understands interest as the faculty between the reason and the passions, a faculty consistent with Patrick Rael's account of early Black uplift oratory and Daniel Howe's account of the Federalist Papers.[20] The inability of Blacks to perceive the workings of the structures that support "wretchedness" is for Walker a sign of African-American inattention to the impulses of interests. In *The Appeal*, this incapacity manifests itself in what Walker shows to be the failure of Black parents to promote the education of their children, in the tendency of Blacks to inform upon each other, and in the ignorant pretension of the masses to literacy.

Black failures to locate their own interests represent for Walker a function of their alienation from a larger social world: the means of communication and dissemination of knowledge within their own communities. For Walker, such knowledge is essential if one is to know why African-Americans ought to oppose the colonization movement, protest the libelous but influential account of Black inferiority in Jefferson's *Notes on the State of Virginia,* and assist in rebellions against Black oppression. At the core of this concern lies Walker's awareness that freedom in a liberal social contract polity is meaningless without the citizen's awareness of his own desires, aims, and resources. And it is such prepolitical knowledge that he seeks for his Black fellows.

Walker's critiques of Black and white life as well as his conceptualizations of "interest" represent only a partial concession to the demands of a social order based upon the pursuit of one's interests. Instead, he does not conceive of a polity whose citizens' virtue emerges from competition. He perhaps naïvely identifies the fulfillment of intelligent self-interest with the inevitable progress of the race. However, the naïveté of this concern reflects not so much a lack of sophistication as Walker's sense of the desperate state of his Black contemporaries' political self-consciousness. Walker seeks a consolidation of social order that will sustain community, political consciousness, and militancy among Blacks. The nearly hysterical response of southern politicians to Walker's *Appeal* points most directly to the way in which it critiques American society and defines Black political interests in terms of a by-then well institutionalized revolutionary discourse.[21] The southerners were only too well aware of the implications of this discourse from the experience of their own political and social ancestors. Significantly there are few if any explicit calls for Black revolution in the *Appeal*; more menacing are its dynamics as revolutionary discourse and Walker's posture as a recognizably American revolutionary hero.

African-Americans of the late eighteenth and early nineteenth centuries acquired an acute political consciousness as they constructed the social realities demanded by their new communities. This political consciousness allowed these early American Blacks to conceptualize their relationship to the various Christian, republican, and Whig ideologies in which the American Revolution had grounded itself. Not only did this consciousness forward a critique of white oppression, it also defined the way in which African-American leaders might exert popular influence and leadership.

Works such as Frederick Douglass's 1845 *Narrative* suggest that the ideologies of Free black societies percolated up to the period's later, more ambitious intellectual works. Much of what the young Douglass has to say about the development of his self-consciousness, his perceptions of the slaves' "interest," as well as his sense of political vocation have already been canvassed in the earlier oratory and essays of the period. These ideological patterns lay also at the bottom of Martin Delaney's character Blake in the novel of that name and the conception of Black community set forth in late nineteenth-century women's novels such as Pauline Hopkins's *Contending Forces*. Implicit in this secularized Black middle-class Protestantism is the central tradition of the first century and a half of African-American writing.

Notes

1. On the white backlash against free black communities, see Leon Laidback, *North of Slavery: The Negro in the Free State 1790–1860* (1966; repr., Chicago: University of Chicago Press, 1961), 98–103; Gary B. Nash, *Forging Freedom: The Formation of Philadelphia's Black Community 1720–1840* (Cambridge, MA: Harvard University Press, 1988), 172–211.

2. On voluntary associations in early Black communities, see, for example, Dorothy Porter, ed., *Early Negro Writing 1760–1837* (Boston: Beacon Press, 1971), 5–8, 79–83, 167–171; Litwack, *North of Slavery*, 17–29, 113–52, 187–213; Nash, *Forging Freedom*, 257–79; William H. Robinson, *Black New England Letters: The Uses of Writing in Black New England* (Boston: Trustees of the Public Library, 1977), 1–25; Ira Berlin and Gary B. Nash, "Forging Freedom: the Emancipation Experience in the Northern Seaport Cities 1775–1820," in *Slavery and Freedom in the Age of the American Revolution*, ed. Ira Berlin and Ronald Hoffman (1983; repr. Urbana: University of Illinois Press, 1986), 43–48.

3. Dorothy Porter, *Early Negro Writing*, 91.

4. For examples of such constitutions, see, for example, Porter, ibid., 9–12, 28–34.

5. For a discussion of early Black schools, see Litwack, *North of Slavery*, 113–52; Patrick Rael, *Black Identity and Black Protest in the Antebellum North* (Chapel Hill: University of North Carolina Press, 2002), 143–146, 189, 113–52. For an example of speakers exhorting Blacks to further education, see Porter, *Early Negro Writing*, 103.

6. Porter, *Early Negro Writing*, 100.

7. William H. Robinson, ed., *Proceedings of the African Union Society and the African Benevolent Society* (Providence, RI: Urban League, n.d.), 145.

8. Robinson, *Proceedings*, 25.

9. Robert A. Ferguson, "William Cullen Bryant: The Creative Context of the Poet," *The New England Quarterly* 53 (December 1980): 436–44.

10. The most convenient source for both of these narratives is Graham Russell Hodges, *Itinerants of the Gospel: The Narratives of John Jea and George White* ((Madison, WI: Madison House, 1993).

11. Vincent Carretta, ed., *Unchained Voices: An Introduction of Black Authors in the English-Speaking World of the 18th Century* (Lexington: University of Kentucky Press, 1996), 325–68.

12. The most convenient and best-documented source for the Marrant narrative is Joanna Brooks and John Saillant, *'Face Zion Forward': First Writers of the Black Atlantic, 1785–1798* (Boston: Northeastern University Press, 2002), 47–176.

13. John Saillant, "Traveling in Old and New Worlds with John Jea, the African Preacher, 1773–1816," *Journal of American Studies* 33 (December 1999): 473–90.

14. My discussion of legitimation and social knowledge draws from Peter L. Berger, "Religion and World Maintenance," in *Sacred Canopy: Elements of a Sociological Theory of Religion* (1990; repr. New York: Doubleday, 1967), 29–51.

15. William L. Andrews, *To Tell a Free Story: The First Century of Afro-American Autobiography: 1760-1865* (Urbana: University of Illinois Press, 1986), 13.

16. David Walker, *David Walker's Appeal: To the Coloured Citizens of the World, but in particular and very expressly, to those of The United States of America* (1829; repr. New York: Hill & Wang), 2.

17. Ibid., 11.

18. Ibid., 22.

19. Ibid., 15.

20. Rael, *Black Identity*, 127–30; Daniel W. Howe, "The Political Psychology of *The Federalist*," *William and Mary Quarterly* 3rd Series, 43, no. 4 (July 1987): 485–509.

21. Peter P. Hinks, *To Awaken My Afflicted Brethren: David Walker and the Problem of Antebellum Resistance* (University Park: Pennsylvania State University Press, 1997), 237–41.

*E*arly African-American Literature?

Let it be remembered, that the nature of things is not altered by our con-
duct. We cannot make truth; it is our business only to find it. No proposi-
tion can become more or less certain or important, by being considered or
neglected.

—Samuel Johnson, Sermon 20

THE USEFULNESS OF IGNORANCE IS UNDERAPPRECIATED. AS
recently as ten years ago, I never imagined that I would ever be
encouraged to contribute an essay to *Aperçus* on the topic of new perspectives on early African-American literature. The invitation is flatter-
ingly ironic. In the mid-1990s I was considered, and considered myself,
an "eighteenth-century scholar," a label everyone in literary studies
understood to mean someone who worked on non-American material. I
had published two books and a number of articles primarily on British
verbal and visual political satire. But early on I showed signs of lacking
discipline. I had crossed some lines in dealing with art and history. In
the eyes of a former colonial Americanist colleague I had committed an
even greater transgression. I had approached Benjamin Franklin and
Paul Revere as British-American rather than exclusively American
satirists. I had gone to my senior colleague to try to talk to him about the

ways Revere used contemporaneous visual English models in his own engraved caricatures. My attempt to have that discussion was rebuffed because my colleague called that approach "un-American" (I assume that he meant un-Americanist). Had I not been so usefully ignorant about intradisciplinary and interdisciplinary boundaries, I would have known enough not to have innocently stumbled upon the subjects of some of my early publications.

Ignorance also led me to the study of the first generation of English-speaking authors of African descent. By the early 1990s I found myself in something of a mid-academic-life crisis, not-quite-consciously searching for something new and exciting to work on. Research projects frequently develop from what one already knows. But working from prior knowledge risks boredom. A less common, but much riskier, way of proceeding is to work on something you do not know, but have reason to believe may be knowable, a procedure I think of as starting from what might be called informed ignorance. You identify a subject you do not know; determine that it is largely unknown to others; and do enough preliminary research to establish that the subject might be mastered. The appeal of such a procedure is the strong risk that, to paraphrase Robert Browning, your scholarly reach may exceed your grasp. Failure is likely; boredom is not.

The resolution of my scholarly crisis began by accident about fifteen years ago. Then as now, I was teaching at the University of Maryland, where a significant percentage of the student body, both undergraduate and graduate, is of African descent. In a nearby bookstore I came across a copy of Henry Louis Gates, Jr.'s recently published anthology entitled *The Classic Slave Narratives*. It reproduces a nineteenth-century edition of *The Interesting Narrative of the Life of Olaudah Equiano, or Gustavus Vassa, the African*, which was first published in London in 1789. Although I had heard of Equiano before then, I had never seen a copy of his work, and from what I had read about it I assumed that it was a text more appropriate for American literature courses than the British courses I was teaching at the time.[1] Everyone I knew assumed that British literature was all-white, all the time. Consequently, any Black anglophone writer was ipso facto African-American. As many other "eighteenth-centuryists" did, I envied my Americanist colleagues because they had authors of African descent they could teach in inexpensive editions. But as soon as I saw that Equiano dedicates his autobiography to the members of the British Parliament I recognized that he had been conceded to the Americanists without a fight. We teachers of British literature did not challenge the placement of Equiano in the tradition of autobiographical writing exemplified by Benjamin Franklin. No one thought to point out that since the publication of Equiano's autobiography preceded that of Franklin's, rather than considering Equiano a Black Franklin we would more accurately call Franklin a white Equiano.

I also recognized immediately when I looked at *The Interesting Narrative* in that College Park bookstore that this should be a very teachable text. The first-person voice was distinctive, and as Equiano says, his "life and fortune" had been "extremely chequered, and [his] adventures various" (236).[2] Categorizing the book as American or African-American literature struck me as more arbitrary than obvious. The author's experiences in North America while a slave were as unpleasant as one might expect. Once he was free, Equiano judged parts of North America reasonably nice places to visit, but he never revealed any interest in voluntarily living there. By Equiano's account, the amount of time he spent in North America during his life could be measured in months, not years. Places where he considered living included Britain, Turkey, and Africa. Ultimately, he chose Britain, in part because Africa was denied him. Hence, I claimed Equiano as one of the earliest African-British authors, thus suitable for my eighteenth-century British literature course. Undergraduates particularly were open to the claim. Usually ignorant of the presumption that he was African-American, they are normally willing to assess the author's self-representation on his own terms. When they learn of the place accorded Equiano in the American and African-American literary canons they are frequently a bit bewildered by the classification.

93

In preparing to teach *The Interesting Narrative* for the first time I began a series of discoveries that have led to my invitation from *Aperçus*. My interest in Equiano was initially solely pedagogical. I did not think that I had much new to say about his autobiography, and I was not attracted to the idea of arguing for his Americanness. But my curiosity was aroused by Gates's choice to reproduce a posthumously published edition of *The Interesting Narrative* rather than one the author himself published. Gates's copy-text first appeared in 1814; Equiano had died in 1797. As everyone else did, I believed that only eight editions of *The Interesting Narrative* had appeared during the author's lifetime, the last in 1794. But I found that a ninth edition had also appeared in 1794, and even more unexpectedly, that the University of Maryland owned one of only two copies of it then known to exist. Two more copies—one in Washington, D.C., and the other in Germany—have subsequently turned up.

Comparison of editions published during Equiano's lifetime with that of 1814 showed that his nineteenth-century editor had altered the text by additions, transpositions, and deletions never made by Equiano himself. Since the only edition of the autobiography available in paperback was based on a corrupted edition published after the author's death, I began to encourage graduate students to produce a critical edition of *The Interesting Narrative* as a dissertation. I also began to lobby publishers to get an authoritative copy into print. I never suggested myself as the editor. Although I was unsuccessful in getting any student to take on the project, one of the presses I had urged to publish an edition of *The Interesting Narrative* eventually asked me whether I would be willing to edit it. Penguin offered me a contract to produce a text for their Classic American literature series. When I objected to classifying the work as narrowly American, Michael Millman at Penguin quickly agreed to publish it instead as a World Classic. He also agreed to let me include every text by Equiano I could find, as well as all the explanatory and textual notes I desired, including the identification of every substantive change Equiano made in each of the nine editions. Never having edited or annotated a primary text before, I was ignorant of what I was getting into. In the process of editing *The Interesting Narrative* I made further discoveries that I never expected, indeed, ones that I had not wanted to make because they so fundamentally challenged my sense of who Olaudah Equiano, or Gustavus Vassa, the African, was.

In retrospect, I was also more ignorant than I should have been about the academic skepticism and resistance I might face in my approach to the task. When a colleague asked me what my next project was going to be and I told her an edition of Equiano's writings, she exclaimed without hesitation, "But *you* don't know anything about Equiano!" Ignoring the insulting implication that I was incapable of knowing a subject I had been quietly studying for several years, I was silently grateful for the unintentional early warning signal. Blissfully unaware of how much work editing involves, I resolved to spend my sabbatical in London, happily digging away in the archives to find the information for my footnotes. Editing provides all the challenge, fun, and frustration of trying to complete a puzzle, many of whose pieces are missing. Later reprintings of the Penguin edition have given me the chance to add new pieces that subsequently came to light, and to correct at least some of my inevitable errors.

As I remind my students, the answers we get depend upon the questions we ask. The questions in turn depend upon how we define or categorize what we are asking about. When I told another Americanist colleague that I was working on Equiano, he said that he taught his autobiography in relation to the role magical realism plays in African-American literary theory. Not being sufficiently versed in the subject I asked him what he was referring specifically to in the text of Equiano's autobiography. He told me that he emphasizes the passage in which, while recounting his participation in an expedition sponsored by the British government to find a passage to the North Pole, Equiano mentions being attacked in a longboat by seahorses. My colleague said that he stresses to his students the significance of the "eruption of the fantastic into the otherwise realistic narrative." I, too, had been struck by the mention of seahorses when I first read that passage, but being unaware of the desirability of finding fantastic eruptions, as an editor I had sought a realistic explanation for the term. My colleague seemed disappointed when I explained that during the eighteenth century arctic walruses were commonly called seahorses. I also showed him a copy of an eighteenth-century print of walruses that was entitled *Seahorses*. Unperturbed by primary evidence, he assured me that he would carry on as before with his theoretical approach to the text.

As far as I could tell, no one who had published on Equiano had systematically tried to establish the verifiability of the many details and dates found in his *Narrative*. As anyone who has looked at his work immediately recognizes, he is remarkably circumstantial in his account of his life, giving far more dates, places, and names, for example, than are found in Franklin's roughly contemporaneous autobiography. This scholarly oversight is very surprising because during the past three decades Olaudah Equiano has become a canonical eighteenth-century figure for historical and literary scholars on both sides of the Atlantic. Excerpts from his autobiography now appear in every anthology and on any Web site covering American, African-American, British, and Caribbean history and literature of the period. The most frequently excerpted sections of his book are from the early chapters on his life in Africa and his experience on the Middle Passage crossing the Atlantic to America. Indeed, it is difficult to think of any historical account of the Middle Passage that does not quote his eyewitness description of its horrors as primary evidence. Before 1985, only the Nigerian critic S. E. Ogude seriously challenged the credibility and reliability of Equiano's memory of Africa. Ogude doubted that a boy who was barely eleven years old at the time could recall so much some thirty years later. But Ogude never questioned Equiano's claim to an African nativity, a claim that was briefly but ineffectively challenged during Equiano's lifetime.[3]

96

The most important and one of the most widely published authors of African descent in the English-speaking world of the eighteenth century, Equiano helped found the genre of the slave narrative when he published The Interesting Narrative. Equiano's work is a spiritual autobiography, captivity narrative, travel book, adventure tale, slavery narrative, economic treatise, apologia, and argument against the transatlantic slave trade and slavery. Equiano says that he was born in 1745, in what is now southeastern Nigeria; kidnapped into slavery around the age of eleven; and then taken to the West Indies. He claims that after a few days on Barbados he was taken to Virginia, where he was sold to a local planter. Michael Henry Pascal, an officer in the British Royal Navy, soon bought him from the planter, renamed him Gustavus Vassa, and took him to London in 1757.

With Pascal, Equiano saw military action during the Seven Years' War. In 1762, as the war drew to a close, Pascal sold him into the horrors of West Indian slavery, rather than freeing him, as Equiano expected. A clever businessman, Equiano saved enough money to buy his own freedom in 1766. The now-free Equiano set off on voyages of commerce and adventure to North America, the Mediterranean, the Middle East, the West Indies, and the North Pole. Returning to London in the early 1770s, he became concerned with spiritual and social reform. He converted to Methodism and in the late 1780s became an outspoken opponent of the slave trade, first in letters to London newspapers, and then in *The Interesting Narrative*. He married an Englishwoman in 1792. One of their two daughters lived to inherit the sizable estate he left at his death on March 31, 1797.

Archival and published records from the period after 1757 attest to Equiano's astoundingly accurate memory of his life. Recent biographical discoveries, however, cast doubt on Equiano's story of his birth and early years. Newly discovered evidence proves that he first reached England in December 1754, a date that would make him significantly younger when he was under Pascal's control than he claims. His baptismal record says that he was born around 1745, while naval records say around 1747. The records agree in locating his birth in South Carolina. If the records are accurate, he invented his African heritage and his much-quoted account of the Middle Passage on a slave ship.[4] The facts that the baptismal and naval records exist were generally less disturbing to scholars than the implications I noted. No one attempted in print to address the implications before *Historically Speaking* published a forum in 2006 on the subject of Equiano's identity.[5] The exchange among the historians Trevor Burnard, Paul Lovejoy, Jon Sensbach, and me gives some idea of what various academic stakeholders have in the question of Equiano's native identity. The implications of questioning his identity are not merely academic. In the United States the Equiano Foundation exists to recognize his achievements; in the United Kingdom the Equiano Society celebrates his contributions; and in Nigeria, particularly among the Igbo, Equiano is a national hero. A person who in many ways was a man without a country for much of his life has become subject to many national claims.

Why had no one else investigated Equiano's naval and other British records? Literary critics are often more interested in the rhetorical aspects and effects of a text than in its historical accuracy. And until very recently, Equiano has been almost exclusively the subject of research by students of American and African-American literature, the relevance of

British naval archives has not been readily apparent. Many historians, on the other hand, often treat published primary texts as transparent, assuming that they have documentary value as uncomplicated utterances. I confess to suspecting that some historians and literary critics, at least subconsciously, may not have wanted to discover that the most often cited account of the Middle Passage might be fictitious. I know that I did not want to. I initially buried my unwelcome findings in footnotes to the first printing of my edition of Equiano's works in 1995. The archival data were completely ignored, as far as I can tell. When I made them public again, this time with a discussion of their possible biographical implications, in *Slavery and Abolition* in 1999, I unintentionally "provoked a list-serve firestorm," to quote a recent reviewer of my biography of Equiano.[6]

Even if Equiano had been born in South Carolina, as his baptismal and naval records say, rather than in Africa, he might still have spoken "no language but that of Africa" when Pascal first met him. Because of the low rate of acculturation of slaves born in Low Country South Carolina during the first half of the eighteenth century, rather than English an African or Creole language was very likely to have been such a slave's first language.[7] Equiano could have been raised during the early years of his life in an essentially exclusively Igbo culture, removed only geographically from its African origins. If he was a native of Carolina, his account of Africa would have been based on secondhand history, oral tradition, and reading rather than on personal experience. The evidence regarding Equiano's place and date of birth is clearly contradictory and will probably remain tantalizingly so. Equiano may have been Igbo-African by descent and early acculturation, African-American by birth, and African British by choice. The possibility of such a complicated answer to the question of Equiano's "true" identity is threatening to some. More than one professional colleague has told me that I should have suppressed the archival evidence. Largely as a result of my research, professional Americanists now disagree about just "how 'American' Equiano's autobiography truly is."[8]

Why might Equiano have invented an African nativity and disguised an American birth? Before 1789 the abundant evidence and many arguments against the transatlantic slave trade were from white voices alone. Initially, opponents of the trade did not recognize the rhetorical power an authentic African voice could wield in the struggle. But Equiano knew that to maintain its increasing momentum the anti–slave trade movement needed precisely the kind of first-person account of Africa and the Middle Passage from the victim's point of view that he could supply. An African, not an African-American, voice was what the abolitionist cause required.

I have spent so much time here on Equiano because he so fully exemplifies the challenge we face in trying to categorize in national terms the first generation of Black writers, most of whom were denied legal and even human identities. Equiano classified himself among the "citizens of the world" (337), an appropriate description of the men and women of African descent who embraced trans- or supranational identities during the eighteenth century when national identities were denied them. Making a virtue of a defect, many of the eighteenth-century writers of African descent resurrected themselves from the social death slavery had imposed on them or their ancestors by assuming a range of available identities. Editing the works of Equiano and those of most of his contemporaries and writing a biography of Equiano have made me recognize that the term *African-British*, though more usefully flexible than *African-American*, is also far too narrow. All of the eighteenth-century Black authors were at least at some point in their lives African-British, either subjects themselves of the British monarch, or legally defined as the property of his subjects. But the end of the American Revolution in 1783 gave these authors the chance for redefinition, either by choice or imposition.[9]

99

No autobiographer faces a greater opportunity for redefinition than a manumitted (freed) slave. Manumission necessitates redefinition. The profoundest possible transformation is the one any slave undergoes when freed, moving from the legal status of property to that of person, from commodity to human being. The former slave is also immediately compelled to redefine himself by choosing a name. Even retention of a slave name is a choice. Choosing not to choose is not an option. With freedom was the obligation to forge a new identity, whether by creating one out of the personal qualities and opportunities at hand, or by counterfeiting one. Equiano may have done both. In one sense, the world lies all before the former slave, who as property had been a person without either a country or a legal personal identity.

None of the people I include in *Unchained Voices: An Anthology of Black Authors in the English-Speaking World of the Eighteenth Century*, for example, is as easily classified in national terms as Frederick Douglass.[10] My title reflects my desire to transcend geographical, national, and political categories. My criteria for inclusion were language, period, and phenotype. Had I conceived of this anthology as one of American or African-American writers only, which of the sixteen should have been included? To answer that question of course we would first have to agree on what we mean by *American*. If the term means anyone who ever spent any time, no matter how brief, in the Western Hemisphere, everyone gets to stay. If we restrict *America* to the part of North America that became the United States, Francis Williams, Ignatius Sancho, and Quobna Ottobah Cugoano have to go. If we remove the authors who chose not to stay or return to live in what became the United States, out go James Albert Ukawsaw Gronniosaw, John Marrant, Equiano, George Liele, David George, and Boston King. As a slave during his whole life, Jupiter Hammon had no choice but to live in America. We do not know whether Briton Hammon lived long enough to have the choice to make. Of our original sixteen authors we would be able to read the written or dictated words of only Phillis Wheatley, Johnson Green, Belinda, Benjamin Banneker, and Venture Smith because they remained in the United States, even though not all did so with equal amounts of enthusiasm. How does one classify writers of African descent like David George and Boston King, who were born in what would become the United States, emigrated to Canada, and moved from there to settle in Africa, where they died? Neither *African-British* nor *African-American* is a category capacious enough to cover all the authors.

Several recently promoted transnational categories are more useful, though each has limitations.[11] Perhaps the best known is the main title of Paul Gilroy's *The Black Atlantic: Modernity and Double Consciousness*.[12] Another category gaining acceptance is the historian Ira Berlin's notion of the "Atlantic creole."[13] Less ethnically restricted transnational categories include *transatlantic* and *circumatlantic*. What all of these transnational categories usefully share is an emphasis on the roles geographical movements of people and culture play in the creation of identities. All of the authors I am concerned with entered the English-speaking world because of forced migration, either during their own lives or those of their ancestors. And most of them crossed the Atlantic in the opposite direction at least once. A transnational approach emphasizes the role that crossing the Atlantic played in the conception, production, distribution, and reception of eighteenth-century Anglophone literature. An overtly transnational approach to the colonial American period would also encourage teachers on both sides of the factitious divide between Americanists and eighteenth-centuryists to try a bit harder to accept the notion that the Atlantic Ocean had two shores. No longer could those of us who teach British literature feel we could ignore Benjamin Franklin. We would all be free to teach any of the authors included in *Unchained Voices*. Equiano could be very productively considered as a man of overlapping, rather than conflicting, identities.

A transnational approach to Black authors would change the way we teach, as well as what we teach. Many of the eighteenth-century authors of African descent have fallen between the cracks in the turf divided by American and British literature specialists: they have been either largely ignored by both camps or claimed by one because of certain characteristics that are emphasized at the expense of others. Americanists would feel free to search for anticipations of Equiano's slave narrative among British precursors, as well as in arguably American models. We should note Joe Snader's observation that "the British captivity tradition, since it deploys the rhetoric of liberty much earlier, much more often, and much more thoroughly than its American counterpart, reveals much closer parallels to the slave narrative and implicates American slavery much more directly."[14] Consequently, the insight of the early-nineteenth-century French critic Henri Grégoire, who compared Equiano to Daniel Defoe's fictional Robinson Crusoe, might be very interestingly elaborated. The significance of the trope of the separated sister found in the narratives of Gronniosaw and Equiano would be explored and pursued in later African-American writings.

In significant and ironic ways a transnational approach to authors of African descent would be a return to the future in the conceptualization of these writers. To Thomas Jefferson and many, if not most, of his contemporaries, the African heritage of such writers subsumed any national claims they might make. Most Americanists are familiar with Thomas Jefferson's notorious comments on Phillis Wheatley in *Notes on the State of Virginia* (London, 1787): "Religion indeed has produced a Phyllis Whately [*sic*]; but it could not produce a poet. The compositions published under her name are beneath the dignity of criticism."[15] But I know very few Americanists, or specialists in British literature for that matter, who recall that Jefferson immediately follows his attack on Wheatley with a much longer and far more ambivalent passage on her Black contemporary on the other side of the Atlantic:

> Ignatius Sancho has approached nearer to merit in composition; yet his letters do more honour to the heart than to the head. They breathe the purest effusions of friendship and general philanthropy, and show how great a degree of the latter may be compounded with strong religious zeal. He is often happy in the turn of his compliments, and his stile is easy and familiar, except when he affects a Shandean fabrication of words. But his imagination is wild and extravagant, escapes incessantly from every restraint of reason and taste, and, in the course of its vagaries, leaves a tract of thought as incoherent and eccentric, as is the course of a meteor through the sky. His subjects should often have led him to a process of sober reasoning: yet we find him always substituting sentiment for demonstration. Upon the whole, though we admit him to the first place among those of his own colour who have presented themselves to the public judgment, yet when we compare him with the writers of the race among whom he lived, and particularly with the epistolary class, in which he has taken his own stand, we are compelled to enroll him at the bottom of the column.[16]

Obviously, anyone interested in trying to understand or teach Jefferson's transnational views on race and literature, as well as the reception history of Wheatley, should feel obligated to be conversant with Sancho's writings, even though Sancho could be categorized as an American author only in the very loosest of senses. He was reportedly born on the Middle Passage and taken to South America before being taken to Britain at the age of two. He never set foot in North America. He opposed slavery and the American Revolution, mockingly referring to George Washington as "Washingtub."[17] Since Jefferson owned a copy of Sancho's *Letters,* published posthumously in 1782, he was well aware of Sancho's comments on Wheatley and her poetry:

> Phyllis's poems do credit to nature—and put art—merely as art—to the blush.—It reflects nothing either to the glory or generosity of her master— if she is still his slave—except he glories in the *low vanity* of having in his wanton power a mind animated by Heaven—a genius superior to himself— the list of splendid—titled—learned names, in confirmation of her being the real authoress.—alas! shews how very poorly the acquisition of wealth and knowledge are—without generosity—feeling—and humanity.—These good great folks—all know—and perhaps admired—nay, praised Genius in bondage—and then, like the Priests and the Levites in sacred writ, passed by—not one good Samaritan amongst them.[18]

A transnational approach would remind us that Wheatley was an African-British author before she adopted an African-American iden-tity, and that her poetry was more popular in England than in America during her lifetime. A transnational approach also changes the context in which we teach early Black writers. When my students read Wheatley's famous October 18, 1773, letter to David Worcester announcing her manumission "at the desire of my friends in England," they usually see her reference to meeting the abolitionist Granville Sharp as far more sig-nificant than the encounter with Franklin she also notes.[19] Sharp had succeeded in inducing Lord Mansfield to rule in 1772 that a slave taken to England could not legally be forced back into colonial slavery. Such a "friend in England" could easily have helped Wheatley pressure her owner to promise to free her if she agreed to return to Boston to care for her ailing mistress.

The approach I am calling for would gain much and lose nothing for Americanists and African Americanists. Equiano would still be taught, but now in a more nuanced and complex way, more fully informed by the contexts in which he wrote, as well as by the traditions out of which his writings emerged. The Americanization of Wheatley during her lifetime, and of Equiano after his death, would be better appreciated. Much that has been ignored because of disciplinary boundaries would be recovered. Even the ways Frederick Douglass, Harriet Jacobs, and W. E. B. Du Bois are taught would need to change. We should spend more time considering them in their transnational contexts. Works like Eliga H. Gould's *The Persistence of Empire*, Joe Snader's *Caught between Worlds*, and Wim Klooster and Alfred Padula, eds., *The Atlantic World* demonstrate the value of using wider contexts for literary studies.[20] Organizations such as the American Society for Eighteenth-Century Studies and the Society of Early Americanists encourage transnational approaches and give them venues in which they can be presented.

A truly transnational and interdisciplinary approach to the first generation of Black authors would render our methodology more precise. We would agree on the primacy of chronology, the fact of change over time, the obligation to consider all available evidence, and the necessity of avoiding reading the present back into the past. We and our students would be prepared to discover that before the nineteenth century neither *race* nor *blackness* was always equivalent to *ethnicity;* that *abolition* and *emancipation* usually did not mean the same thing; and that an Englishwoman could be described as being Black with a peaches and cream complexion. Among many other surprises, our students would discover that Africans played a crucial role in the establishment and maintenance of the transatlantic slave trade, that only a relatively small percentage of enslaved Africans were taken to North America, that many enslaved people were not born into slavery, that not all slaves worked on plantations, and that before the last quarter of the eighteenth century most people saw slavery as an economic rather than a moral issue. We must be careful to acknowledge differences as well as similarities, lest we sound as if we are attempting to "Americanize" all culture produced by people of African descent. Some Americanists, for example, lay claim to any literature produced in the Americas as part of the American (i.e., United States) tradition. To many of our fellow Americans (i.e., residents of countries in the Americas other than the United States) such appropriation is simply a form of cultural imperialism.

Fortunately, the literary turf fights have greatly diminished in number and ferocity in the wake of the development of Black Atlantic and transatlantic Anglophone studies. Those of us who want to work on both sides of the water without overreaching live in encouraging times. We can follow the paths our useful ignorance leads us to without being discouraged by the willful ignorance that defines some lines of investigation as out of bounds.

Notes

1. Although the author of *The Interesting Narrative* almost always referred to himself in public and private by his legal name, Gustavus Vassa, given him in slavery, he is best known today as Olaudah Equiano, the identity he claims in his autobiography.

2. All quotations from Equiano's works are taken from Vincent Carretta, ed., *The Interesting Narrative and Other Writings*, 2nd ed. (New York: Penguin Putnam, 2003), and are cited by page number parenthetically within the text.

3. S. E. Ogude, "Facts into Fiction: Equiano's *Narrative* Reconsidered," *Research in African Literatures* 13 (1982): 30–43. Ogude argues that because an eleven-year-old was very unlikely to have the almost total recall Equiano claims, "Equiano relied less on the memory of his experience and more on other sources" (32) in his account of Africa. Arguments supporting the accuracy of Equiano's memory of Africa appear in Catherine Obianju Acholonu, "The Home of Olaudah Equiano—a Linguistic and Anthropological Search," *Journal of Commonwealth Literature* 22 (1987): 5–16; and Paul Edwards and Rosalind Shaw, "The Invisible *Chi* in Equiano's *Interesting Narrative*," *Journal of Religion in Africa* 19 (1989): 146–56; Acholonu, *The Igbo Roots of Olaudah Equiano* (Owerri, Nigeria: Ata, 1989), identifies "Essaka" as modern-day Isseke, near Ihiala, Nigeria, and claims she has found Equiano's direct descendants. But since her argument requires us to believe that her sources lived to be more than 150 years old, her methodology is suspect. In "No Roots Here: On the Igbo Roots of Olaudah Equiano," *Review of English and Literary Studies* 5 (1989): 1–16, Ogude denies that linguistic evidence supports Equiano's account. G. I. Jones, "Olaudah Equiano of the Niger Ibo," in *Africa Remembered: Narratives by West Africans from the Era of the Slave Trade* ed. Philip D. Curtin, 60–69 (Madison: University of Wisconsin Press, 1967), finds Equiano's account of his "home and travels in Nigeria . . . disappointingly brief and confused." He believes that "the little he can remember of his travels is naturally muddled and incoherent" because Equiano "was only eleven years old when he was kidnapped" (61, 69). In her review of Paul Edwards, *The Life of Olaudah Equiano*, and Acholonu, "The Igbo Roots of Olaudah Equiano," *Journal of African History*, 33 (1992): 164–65, Elizabeth Isichei remarks of Equiano's description of Africa, "I have come to believe that it is a palimpsest, and that though he was indeed an Igbo (though even this has been questioned) he fused his own recollections with details obtained from other Igbo into a single version" (165). Katherine Faull Eze, "Self-Encounters: Two Eighteenth-Century African Memoirs from Moravian Bethlehem," in *Crosscurrents: African Americans, Africa, and Germany in the Modern World* ed. David McBride, LeRoy Hopkins, and C. Aisha Blackshire-Belay, 29–52 (Columbia, SC: Camden House, 1998), considers "Equiano's Igbo past [to be] mostly a reconstruction of European or Colonial American travel narratives, most obviously, Anthony Benezet's *Some Historical Account of Guinea*," 33, 50n22.

4. See my "Questioning the Identity of Olaudah Equiano, or Gustavus Vassa, the African," in *The Global Eighteenth Century*, ed. Felicity Nussbaum, 226–35 (Baltimore: Johns Hopkins University Press, 2003).

5. *Historically Speaking: The Bulletin of the Historical Society* 7 (2006): 2–16.

6. Joanna Pope Melish, review of Vincent Carretta, *Equiano the African: Biography of a Self-Made Man*, *American Historical Review* 111 (2006): 795–96; quotation on 796.

7. Philip D. Morgan, *Slave Counterpoint: Black Culture in the Eighteenth-Century Chesapeake and Lowcountry* (Chapel Hill: University of North Carolina Press, 1998), 465.

105

8. Rafia Zafar, *We Wear the Mask: African Americans Write American Literature, 1760–1870* (New York: Columbia University Press, 1997), 207.

9. See Vincent Carretta, *Equiano, the African: Biography of a Self-Made Man* (Athens: University of Georgia Press, 2005); Simon Schama, *Rough Crossings: Britain, the Slaves and the American Revolution* (New York: Ecco, 2006); Cassandra Pybus, *Epic Journeys of Freedom: Runaway Slaves of the American Revolution and Their Global Quest for Liberty* (Boston: Beacon Press, 2006); Christopher Leslie Brown, *Moral Capital: Foundations of British Abolitionism* (Chapel Hill: University of North Carolina Press, 2006).

10. Vincent Carretta, ed., *Unchained Voices: An Anthology of Black Authors in the English-Speaking World of the Eighteenth Century,* 2nd ed. (Lexington: University Press of Kentucky, 2004).

11. Allison Games, "Atlantic History: Definitions, Challenges, and Opportunities," *American Historical Review* 111 (2006): 741–57, provides a bibliography as well as a useful survey of the various positions and the state of the field.

12. Paul Gilroy, *The Black Atlantic: Modernity and Double Consciousness* (Cambridge, MA: Harvard University Press, 1993).

13. Ira Berlin, "From Creole to African: Atlantic Creoles and the Origins of African-American Society in Mainland North America," *The William and Mary Quarterly*, 3rd series 53, no. 2 (1996): 251–88.

14. Joe Snader, *Caught between Worlds: British Captivity Narratives in Fact and Fiction* (Lexington: University Press of Kentucky, 2000), 281.

15. Jefferson's misspelling of Wheatley's name was probably due to his reliance on his aural rather visual memory. He probably did not have his copy of her *Poems* with him in France when he wrote his *Notes.* During the eighteenth century, *eat* and *ate* were both pronounced like the modern *ate.*

16. Frank Shuffleton, ed. Thomas Jefferson, *Notes on the State of Virginia* (New York: Penguin Putnam, 1999), 147–48.

17. Vincent Carretta, ed. Ignatius Sancho, *Letters of the Late Ignatius Sancho, an African* (New York: Penguin Putnam, 1998), 106.

18. Sancho, *Letters,* 112.

19. Vincent Carretta, ed. Phillis Wheatley, *Complete Writings* (New York: Penguin Putnam, 2001), 147.

20. Eliga H. Gould, *The Persistence of Empire: British Political Culture in the Age of the American Revolution* (Chapel Hill: University of North Carolina Press, 2000); Wim Klooster and Alfred Padula, eds., *The Atlantic World: Essays on Slavery, Migration, and Imagination* (New York: Prentice Hall, 2004).

Philip Gould

'Early Black Atlantic Writing and the Cultures of Enlightenment

SINCE THE 1960s AND 1970s THE FIELD OF AFRICAN-AMERICAN literary studies has developed to the point where it no longer can be seen as marginal to American literary studies. Critics now recognize how important the field is to a full account of American literary history. But the course of African-American studies' emergence has led to a kind of historical imbalance, emphasizing the antebellum slave narrative and its influence on nineteenth- and twentieth-century African-American literature, particularly the novel. The central place of the relation between slave narrative and novel is not surprising. Pioneers in the field understandably tried to legitimize it according to many of the same priorities that dominated literary studies in general, and so the field's development demanded that one show the merits of Black fiction, poetry, and drama. Yet these professional and institutional pressures have produced narratives of African-American literary history that generally start in the 1830s and 1840s. This has led to eliding or undervaluing the importance of eighteenth-century Black writing in general. How do we recover this earlier writing on its own terms? How can we reimagine new kinds of literary histories that move "beyond Douglass"?[1]

The field's relatively modern center of gravity perhaps inevitably tends to read the antebellum period "backward" onto the eighteenth century. By that I mean that, until recently, eighteenth-century writers like Olaudah Equiano have been read as precursors for the antebellum slave narrative. Although there are important connections between eighteenth-century and antebellum literature—the prevalence of auto-biographical discourses, for example—early Black writing demonstrates many distinctive features that may be understood in contexts associated with the eighteenth-century "Enlightenment." Besides being unwieldy, however, this category generally has elicited backlash from scholars against Eurocentric thinking.

Let me briefly illustrate this critical antagonism to a Eurocentric Enlightenment by calling forth two prominent scholarly works that have been influential in the field. In *Figures in Black: Words, Signs, and the "Racial" Self* (1987), for example, Henry Louis Gates Jr. argued for fundamental importance of print literacy to Enlightenment conceptions of humanity, a fact that resulted in highly politicized debates about the "nature" of Africans as well as Black writers' self-consciousness about authenticating themselves for largely white audiences. The most egregious example of the Eurocentric Enlightenment's predilection for consigning Africans to perpetual barbarity has been the infamous example of the disparaging remarks Thomas Jefferson made in *Notes on the State of Virginia* (1785) about the well-known poet Phillis Wheatley. As Gates has argued, even those enlightened critics who emphasized the importance of environmental factors on race only managed to distort criticism about African-American writing in general and Wheatley in particular: "Metonymically . . . her relation to the potential of other black people to assume 'cultivation' remained consistent in critical writings well into the twentieth century, in part because of Jefferson's use of her as the written record of the sum total of the African's potential for 'civilization,' followed by the manifestly felt need of blacks and their sympathizers to refute Jefferson's claims."[2]

In *The Black Atlantic: Modernity and Double Consciousness* (1993) Paul Gilroy offered an even more trenchant critique of the Enlightenment legacy. Faulting Western narratives about the rise of modernity for separating the Enlightenment from the brutal histories of race and slavery, Gilroy reinserts those histories into it as a way of reconstructing a counterhistory of modernity. Adapting Hegelian theory of the master-slave relation, Gilroy argues that the Eurocentric ideals about freedom were made possible only in terms of "the brute facts of modern slavery." By accounting for a "primal history of modernity" from the point of view of Black slaves, we can begin to "rethink the meanings of rationality, autonomy, reflection, subjectivity, and power in light of an extended meditation both on the condition of the slaves and on the suggestion that racial terror is not merely compatible with occidental rationalism but cheerfully complicit with it."[3] Gilroy's overall project of dismantling rigid models of race is in large part motivated by undermining the Enlightenment legacy. While admitting that Black writers historically have straddled "the grand narrative of Enlightenment and its operational principles," and ambivalently situated themselves vis-à-vis a "western culture which has been their peculiar step-parent," the most potent forms of Black Atlantic writing have tended to challenge the reductive categories of this culture, which have denied the contingency and fluidity of all subject formations (48–49).

My understanding of early Black writing's relation to Enlightenment ideologies is generally more benign than this. These ideologies are in many ways more elastic than Gilroy allows. By recasting the relation between Black authorship and Enlightenment ideology, we might be able to relocate early Black Atlantic writing culturally outside the traditional dichotomy between complicity and resistance. In the following, I address features of Enlightenment culture that may have been simultaneously empowering and troubling to early Black writers: the importance of individual rights, benevolent humanitarianism, the importance of experience and observation, the belief in progressive history, and Christian evangelicalism, especially its emphasis on conversion and reform. These discourses inform early Black writing's ideological interventions in the "Enlightenment." By reconsidering early Black writing's historical relation to these discourses, moreover, we can begin to redraw the larger thematic and rhetorical patterns in Black Atlantic literary history from the 1760s to the 1860s.

∾

One place to start in redrawing these relations might be eighteenth-century sentimentalism. Not only did sentimental discourse empower eighteenth-century writers like Equiano and Wheatley to argue against slavery and legitimize themselves as writers, but its legacy is also felt in the antebellum slave narrative. Let me begin to show the importance of eighteenth-century sentimental categories on the antebellum slave narrative by focusing on a well-known (and I suspect often taught) scene in the *Narrative of the Life of Frederick Douglass, an American Slave* (1845). The *Narrative*'s opening chapter concludes with Douglass's recollection of the horror he felt while witnessing his master's merciless whipping of Aunt Hester. Douglass frames the scene carefully: it displays in detail the process of binding her and stripping her nearly naked, so that the whipping captures the subtle connections between sexual desire and patriarchal violence at the heart of white mastery. "After crossing her hands, he tied them with a strong rope, and led her to a stool under a large hook. She now stood fair for his infernal purpose."[4] The most important narrative technique here is the positioning of the reader vis-à-vis the abused slave woman and the young boy who witnesses her, both of which are mediated by the designs of the narrator Douglass disguised merely as recollection.

110

The overall technique of the scene cannot help but recall the famous opening of Adam Smith's highly influential treatise *The Theory of Moral Sentiments* (1759), which was widely read in the early American republic. Smith's analysis of the exchange of feeling between the witness and subject of distress—that between Douglass's reader, for example, and Aunt Hester, or even between that reader and Douglass himself—articulates the delicate balance between intimacy and distance that later will be crucial to the slave narrative genre. "As we have no immediate experience of what other men feel, we can form no idea of the manner in which they are affected, but by conceiving what we ourselves should feel in the like situation. Though our brother is upon the rack, as long as we ourselves are at our ease, our senses will never inform us of what he suffers. . . . By the imagination we place ourselves in his situation, we conceive ourselves enduring all the same torments, we enter as it were into his body, and become in some measure the same person with him."[5] I have italicized the phrase *in some measure* because it suggests the qualified and perhaps ambivalent form of sentimental identification between Black subjects and white readers (or listeners) that the slave narrative creates. This scene enforces and yet withdraws from that identification.

The narrative control that Douglass exhibits in displaying the visual spectacle of plantation violence (a private crime made public) positions the reader just close enough to be horrified and yet safely distant enough to maintain (perhaps as Douglass did himself) the capacity to analyze it rationally. Readers can only feel what they are able to imagine for themselves, and they can imagine only by remaining removed. Thus the visual scene concludes not only with Aunt Hester's pitiful screams and dripping blood but also with the master's "savage" profanity—the idea that that slavery reduces whites too to brutes and that our understanding of racial categories of civilization and savagery is not what it once was.

If this moment in the *Narrative* begins to suggest the empowering potential of the Enlightenment legacy, it also emphasizes another important continuity between eighteenth-century and antebellum antislavery cultures: the central role of the family in producing sympathy. The examples of this in eighteenth-century writings and speeches are widespread. Slaves petitioning for their freedom, for example, often gave mini-autobiographies emphasizing the horrors of their experiences in captivity. In 1774, for example, a group of slaves in Massachusetts petitioning the royal governor complained of the loss of their children, who "were dragged from their mother's breast." Later, in 1782, Belinda's "Petition of an African Slave, to the Legislature of Massachusetts" (which was later published in early American magazines) employed the same kind of strategy.[6] Eighteenth-century slave narratives similarly emphasized the slave trade's destruction of African families. One finds it in *The Interesting Narrative of the Life of Olaudah Equiano, or Gustavus Vassa* (1789), especially where he emphasizes familial feeling in Benin and the subsequent horror of the Middle Passage.

The antebellum slave narrative's emphasis on the destruction of families, then, must be seen in light of a long literary tradition that emphasizes the full humanity of Africans. The obvious place to reconsider this crucial theme in the antebellum canon would be Harriet Jacobs's *Incidents in the Life of a Slave Girl* (1861). Indeed *Incidents* might be read as an extended meditation on this longstanding theme. Writers like Jacobs certainly had available to them fully developed domestic discourses, which were dominant in other genres and print media by the 1850s. Yet the slave narrative's sentimental treatment of familial crisis

111

just as significantly recalls eighteenth-century ideas and writings. Readers, for example, often overlook the fact that Jacobs's famous chapter "The Loophole of Retreat" is an allusion to the eighteenth-century British poet William Cowper's *The Task* (1784), which was widely popular (and often reprinted) in nineteenth-century America. This transatlantic reading of antebellum works, moreover, involves not only thematic connections but also stylistic resemblances. The latter are particularly felt in the popular abolitionist poetry that was published in broadsides and in antislavery magazines and newspapers and anthologized in antislavery annuals.

Compare, for example, the opening of Cowper's famous antislavery poem "The Negro's Complaint" (1787), which was published and republished extensively on both sides of the Atlantic, with the concluding stanzas of Frances Ellen Watkins Harper's "The Slave Mother" (1854).

> Forced from home and all its pleasures
>> Afric's coast I left forlorn,
> To increase a stranger's treasures
>> O'er the raging billows borne;
> Men from England bought and sold me,
>> Pay'd my price in paltry gold;
> But, though slave they have enroll'd me
>> Minds are never to be sold.

And Harper:

> They tear him from her circling arms,
>> Her last and fond embrace.
> Oh! Never more may her sad eyes
>> Gaze on his mournful face.
> No marvel, then, these bitter shrieks
>> Disturb the listening air:
> She is a mother, and her heart
>> Is breaking in despair.[7]

While Harper's verse cannot be reduced thematically to popular models such as Cowper's, the comparison does begin to explain the aesthetic choices she makes. In light of the continued popularity in nineteenth-century America of poets like Cowper, Harper's highly formalized verse was working within proven literary conventions. The rhyme scheme, metrical rhythm, Victorian language all work to place her in a respectable "literary" culture as well as antislavery politics, and these literary conventions also help to control the emotional and physical violence her indictment of the African slave trade produces.

Early Black writers, however, encountered particular difficulties in managing sentimental discourse. One should keep in mind that both historians and literary critics traditionally have been quite skeptical about the authenticity of antislavery sentiment.[8] Perhaps critics in the field have undervalued both the rhetorical leverage and the ideological problems that antislavery sentiment afforded Black writing. It posed at least two major challenges for early Black writers. One was that sentimental language often implies the lack of difference; it tends to subsume racial or gendered differences, for example, within the trope of "humanity" that itself registers Enlightenment tendencies to seek out universal categories of analysis. The second problem oddly derives from the first: sentimentalizing the horrors of slavery often led to the narrative erasure of Africans themselves, usually in violent death or even tragic suicide. The prototype for this representational strategy is Thomas Day's famous poem *The Dying Negro* (1773), which recounts, through an imagined African speaker, all the horrors of slavery and the slave trade—only to kill off the suffering slave finally through melodramatic suicide. Countless poems, vignettes, and sketches staging slave suicides in the eighteenth century were the literary materials bestowed on later former slave autobiographers. They were faced with the difficulty of sentimentally connecting with white readers while refusing to reduce Black suffering to simplistic formulas.

The importance of sentimental culture clarifies as well the prominent role of religion in so much of early Black writing. Indeed we cannot read a good deal of this writing—Phillis Wheatley's poetry, for example, or the work of Briton Hammon, Jupiter Hammon, Prince Hall, Lemuel Haynes, and John Marrant—without acknowledging the central place of Christianity in their work. We have to let go of secular bias if we are to bring into focus the rhetorical and thematic relations between these early writers and later figures like Sojourner Truth, Jarena Lee, and Zilpha Elaw. Numerous religious motifs pervade early Black auto-biography and attune literary representation: the persona of the pious soul, the quest for grace and spiritual conversion, dreams and visions, the racial politics of spiritual emancipation, and Christian humanitarianism that segues easily into meditations on the civilization/barbarity opposition and into moral critiques of slavery and racism. Such pervasiveness does not politically neuter this writing; rather the boundaries between spiritual and temporal conceptions of freedom become hopelessly confused so that each animates and invigorates the other. Consider, for example, Wheatley's famous letter to the Mohegan minister Samson Occom, which was published in a Connecticut newspaper in 1774. Likening the "Egyptian bondage" of the ancient Israelites to the condition of contemporary Africans, Wheatley declares, "For in every human breast, God has implanted a Principle, which we call Love of Freedom; it is impatient of Oppression, and pants for Deliverance; and by the Leave of our modern Egyptians, I will assert, that same principle lives in us."

114   The religious tradition of early Black writing has further ramifications for gender, especially regarding Black writers who later felt compelled to redefine the terms of Black masculinity. The means of brokering thematic compromises between Black masculinity and evangelical Christianity were often stressful and never simple. This was especially true after the publication of *Uncle Tom's Cabin* (1852), a work that Black abolitionists admired and yet resisted, largely because of Stowe's feminization of the ideal Black man. While some simply rejected Christian pacifism, most intervened more creatively to incorporate Christian feeling into acts of slave resistance. Surely, antislavery fiction like Douglass's *The Heroic Slave* (1853) and Martin Delany's *Blake; or, The Huts of America* (1859) was responding in part to Stowe's novel, but it also should be read in light of evangelical motifs in early Black literature that often emphasized the importance of Christian submission. Reading *Blake* in light of the work of Briton Hammon or Jupiter Hammon, for example, demonstrates the historical scope of this novel's objections. It not only widens the historicity of that novel but puts pressure on the very notion of a unified Black literary tradition.

     The subject of property provided another context for Black writing's ongoing project of affirming Black humanity. The autobiographical preoccupation with the issue of property was thoroughly enmeshed in Enlightenment ideas about labor, value, and property rights. In the eighteenth century, these ideas derived in large part from Locke's theories of property rights, and proslavery apologists were quick to utilize these ideas to defend the institution. Early Black writers were sensitive to the terms in which these debates were waged, and so it is no surprise that many engaged the subject of African humanity on such terms. This is apparent, for example, in James Forten's famous *Letters from a Man of Color* (1813), a work protesting Pennsylvania legislation meant to reduce the state's Black population. "Many of us," Forten complained, "are men of property, for the security of which, we have hitherto looked to the laws of our blessed state, but should this become a law, our property is jeopardized, since the same power which can expose to sale an unfortunate fellow creature, can wrest from him those estates, which years of honest industry have accumulated."[9]

But early Black writing also was capable of revising this correlation of humanity with property. A contemporary of Forten's, for example, Daniel Coker, who was minister of the African Methodist Episcopal Church in Baltimore, published *A Dialogue Between a Virginian and an African Minister*, a work whose form was likely influenced by Samuel Hopkins's famous *Dialogue on Slavery* (1776). Responding to the Virginian's claim to his property rights, the minister explains that Africans were converted from men into property by unjust laws that violated "the law of humanity, common sense, reason, and conscience": "But the question is concerning the liberty of a man. The man himself claims it as his own property . . . by the common laws of justice and humanity, it is still his own."[10] Long before the rise of the antebellum slave narrative, then, Black writers were self-conscious about disentangling the terms of Black humanity from traditional property rights. Yet there is no formula for reading this writing's rhetorical strategies, and no set standard for judging its rhetorical success. Writers like Coker were largely successful in making an ethical case for natural rights, but, as one can see in the preceding passage, even his defense suggests that liberty *itself* is a form of property. This problem was compounded in autobiographical writings where slave narrators like Equiano and Venture Smith were forced to work—to earn property—in order to purchase their liberty. On the one hand, then, staging the virtue of Black labor went far in undermining racial stereotypes about the nature of Africans; on the other, it operated within basic Lockean assumptions that potentially reduced Africans to the property they could acquire.

This provides an important context for seeing the directions nineteenth-century African-American writing takes. This writing often turned to other kinds of ideological footholds than property rights as a way of denouncing slavery. By the 1830s and 1840s, it certainly became easier to critique the moral equivalence of property and humanity. This often led to detailed analysis of the economics of slavery that oscillated between the tonal poles of sincere outrage and ironic bemusement. Compare, for example, the opening paragraphs of *Incidents in the Life of a Slave Girl* with the "Economy" section that begins *Walden* (1854). Each work juxtaposes the material economy of slave capitalism with the moral and spiritual economies that ideally regulate our behavior, thus exposing the absurdity of modern society's reduction of human beings to material things. In his important antislavery novel *Clotel; or the President's Daughter* (1853), William Wells Brown employs much the same strategy when, for example, the sale of Thomas Jefferson's illegitimate children spark's the narrator's moral outrage. By the antebellum period the separation of the Lockean integration of property and humanity was a standard convention of antislavery literature (and indeed other kinds of reform writing as well), with the slave's "bill of sale" symbolizing the dehumanization of slave capitalism.

The uses to which eighteenth-century Black Atlantic writers put Enlightenment ideology also include their rhetorical management of the crucial categories of "liberty" and "slavery." Decoding this language in early Black writing is one of the great joys and challenges of reading and teaching this literature. That is because during the eighteenth century these terms signified on many different registers that in practice inevitably overlapped—political, economic, psychological, religious, and even sexual. Classical Whig writing, for example, in eighteenth-century Britain usually harangued readers about the conspiracies being hatched by corrupt politicians and financiers who were plotting to further their own interests and make "slaves" of supposedly free Englishmen—to reduce them to servile beings robbed of an independent will. Many historians of the American Revolutionary period have shown how influential this

Whig tradition was during the 1760s and 1770s as scores of colonial pamphleteers warned Americans about the dangers of enslavement.

The political context for slavery was important for Black writing produced in an age of revolutions. And it was especially true in revolutionary America, where the ethical inconsistencies of a slaveholding republic emerged. How could Americans, antislavery writers (many of them Black) suggest, argue for natural rights in the face of British "slavery" while they continued to practice slave keeping and slave trading at home? This situation created for the antislavery imagination a host of highly ironic comparisons between "enslaved" Africans and Americans. The fact that the discourses of chattel and political slavery so easily overlapped and often chafed against each other made it relatively easy for early Black writing to point out the hypocrisy of revolutionary language and ideals. Rather than disposing of this morally bankrupt language, however, Black writing generally revitalized it and went on to redeploy revolutionary republican discourses about rights and liberty. The *locus classicus* for this rhetorical approach is of course Benjamin Banneker's famous letter to Thomas Jefferson pleading the case of enslaved African-Americans in republican America. Banneker does not merely suggest Jefferson's own moral culpability but does so by using the very language of the Declaration itself. Thus begins in earnest one of the most important trends in American antislavery writing from the 1770s to the Civil War: the ability of Black writers to reappropriate the Declaration of Independence and transform it into a foundational antislavery document.

The increasing racialization of slavery in the antebellum period only intensified such rhetorical approaches. In the nineteenth century Black writing continued to rely upon the cultural power of both Christian and republican discourses. One reliable strategy for countering pseudoscientific racial theories about the innate inferiority of Africans was to emphasize the traditional Christian account of the origins of humanity found in the Bible. Another was to draw upon Enlightenment theory about natural rights and the republican discourses that articulated them. If Black petitioners during the American Revolution "imbibed the ideology of natural and inalienable rights,"[11] antebellum Black writers demonstrate with equal force the enduring cultural legacy of the revolutionary founding. One of the obvious places one sees this is in Douglass's novella *The Heroic Slave* (1853), where the protagonist, Madison Washington, often functions as a ventriloquist for the popular language of revolutionary history (Douglass did point out the moral problems with this language in his famous speech delivered in Rochester, New York, "What to the Slave Is the Fourth of July?"). Revolutionary ideology and language were not confined to writers like Douglass but circulated widely among antebellum anti-slavery writers and informs, for example, less canonical works like William Nell's *The Colored Patriots of the American Revolution* (1855).

Eighteenth-century ideas about the importance of "manners" also helped to shape the language of early Black writing. Eighteenth-century culture understood the concept of manners quite broadly; it was associated with theories of historical development and seen to be crucial to modern commercial societies. The importance cultural critics placed on the virtues of civility and politeness helped to define the difference between "civilization" and "savagery." Early Black writers like Francis Williams and Phillis Wheatley accessed these virtues as they poetically fashioned themselves. Later Black writing continues to oppose the developing opposition between whiteness and blackness with this alternative one between civilization and savagery rooted in Enlightenment conceptions of civilized manners. This was a powerful rhetorical resource for the slave narrative and the antislavery novel. When Douglass, for example, gives his famous definition of slavery as "darkening his mental and moral condition," he is drawing on this cultural tradition of enlightened manners. Slave narrators were highly self-conscious about upholding their civilized identities, even in moments of violent opposition to slavery. Even white abolitionists like William Lloyd Garrison—whose racial views were at best problematic—attacked "American Colorphobia" as demonstrating the absence of civility and manners. On both fronts, slave narrative and abolitionist writing were trying to counter racial understandings of slavery by returning to this moral and cultural tradition rooted in Enlightenment discourses of "civilization."

∾

Some very basic features of Enlightenment ideology—the value of sentiment, its relation to evangelical piety, the importance of civility and manners, the ongoing preoccupation with natural rights—were crucial to early Black writing. These principles were not immediately accessible to people of African descent. But eighteenth-century writers and relaters did access them. By inserting themselves in Enlightenment culture, moreover, they altered the contours of that culture and changed the way it looks to us today. In this context, antebellum African-American literature also takes on a different appearance. Instead of reading antebellum works as precursors to modern African-American literature, we might begin to consider them as part of an Enlightenment historical legacy constituting not a seamless tradition but a period from the 1760s to 1860s that was characterized by points of continuity as well as transformative change.

The paradigm of the Black Atlantic puts pressure on national models of literary and cultural analysis so that teaching "African-American" literature becomes somewhat more problematic. The passage to Britain (and back to America) influenced the careers of early writers like Phillis Wheatley and John Marrant long before antebellum abolitionists like 119 Douglass made this influential journey. When antebellum Black writers used this experience to point out the irony of the moral superiority of Great Britain to the supposedly republican United States, they were not inventing but pushing harder on an existing rhetorical trope. One important factor that often goes unnoticed is the place of British antislavery activism in the African-American historical imagination. Ever since the 1780s, when the English Abolition Society was formed, Black writers held up Granville Sharp, William Wilberforce, and Thomas Clarkson as heroic models of the humanitarian cause. Such hagiography describes such works as Joseph Holly's poetry collection *Freedom's Offering* (1853) and the work being published in influential Black newspapers and periodicals.

This transatlantic context for Black writing expands our sense of the representational world of the slave narrative. Reading—and teaching—"beyond Douglass" begins to displace the central place of the southern plantation, where nearly mythic scenes like Douglass's battle with Covey the slave breaker take place. The transatlantic antislavery imagination included many crucial points where the brutality of commerce and labor occurred: the Gold Coast, the Bight of Biafra, and other slave trading centers along the West African littoral, where the "savage trade" of human beings was conducted; the misery of the Middle Passage; the slave-trading seaports of British America; and the barbarity of the West Indian plantation, where the world's "blood sugar" was cultivated. In the late eighteenth century antislavery writing located the West Indies as the place where English planters lost civilized English identities. In the nineteenth century, especially after British emancipation in 1833, the American South took over that kind of cultural role. The longer historical view as well as the transatlantic scope of a course in the early Black Atlantic shows students how and why one image easily was superimposed on another, since each was meant to represent the corruption, lassitude, sham piety, and unregulated passions of slave society. As the locus of that corruption, the southern plantation actually inscribes representational motifs that reach beyond the antebellum slave narrative and the U.S. nation as well.

Notes

1. See, for example, Robert Bone, *The Negro Novel in America* (New Haven, CT: Yale University Press, 1958) and *Down Home: Origins of the Afro American Short Story* (New York: Putnam, 1975); Addison Gayle, *Bondage, Freedom, and Beyond: The Prose of Black Americans* (Garden City, NY: Zenith, 1971) and *The Way of the New World: The Black Novel in America* (Garden City, NY: Anchor, 1975); Charles Nichols, *Many Thousands Gone: The Ex-Slave's Account of Their Bondage and Freedom* (Bloomington: Indiana University Press, 1969); Charles Scruggs, *Sweet Home: Invisible Cities in the Afro-American Novel* (Baltimore: Johns Hopkins University Press, 1993); and Robert Stepto, *From behind the Veil: A Study of Afro-American Narrative* (Urbana: University of Illinois Press, 1979). More recent studies that are structured according to the antebellum slave narrative's seminal influence include Hazel Carby, *Reconstructing Womanhood: The Emergence of the Afro-American Woman Novelist* (New York: Oxford University Press, 1987); Valerie Smith, *Self-Discovery and Authority in Afro-American Narrative* (Cambridge, MA: Harvard University Press, 1987); and Eric Sundquist, *To Wake the Nations: Race in the Making of American Literature* (Cambridge, MA: Harvard University Press, 1993).

2. *Figures in Black: Words, Signs, and the "Racial" Self* (New York: Oxford, 1987), 73.

3. *The Black Atlantic: Modernity and Double Consciousness* (Cambridge, MA: Harvard University Press, 1993), 55–56.

4. *Narrative of the Life of Frederick Douglass, an American Slave* (New York: Penguin, 1986), 52.

5. Adam Smith, *The Theory of Moral Sentiments*, ed. D. D. Raphael and A. L. Macfie, 9 (Indianapolis: Liberty, 1984).

6. See Vincent Carretta, ed., *Unchained Voices: An Anthology of Black Authors in the English-Speaking World of the 18th Century* (Lexington: University Press of Kentucky, 1997), 142–43.

7. Both of these poems have been reprinted in *The Poetry of Slavery: An Anglo-American Anthology, 1764–1865* ed. Marcus Wood, 91–92, 603–4, (New York: Oxford University Press, 2003).

8. See, for example, Winthrop Jordan's White *over Black: American Attitudes towards the Negro, 1550-1812* (Chapel Hill: University of North Carolina Press, 1968), which dismissed the antislavery feeling of white reformers as not only mawkish but narcissistic, an argument that has stuck resiliently to the historical reputation of American abolitionists.

9. James Forten, *Letters from a Man of Color* (Philadelphia, 1813), 2.

10. Daniel Coker, *A Dialogue between a Virginian and an African Minister* (Baltimore: Benjamin Edes, 1810), 6.

11. Gary B. Nash, *Forging Freedom: The Formation of Philadelphia's Black Community, 1720–1840* (Cambridge, MA: Harvard University Press, 1988), 58.

John Saillant

$\mathcal{A}$spirant Citizenship

BLACK MEN AND BLACK WOMEN BEGAN WRITING IN ENGLISH
and publishing their works in a momentous era in American thought.
The years from 1760 to 1830—the time of the genesis of African-
American literature, religion, and social thought—saw clear expressions
of some of the salient ideas and values of the Euro-American past as well
as articulations of innovative notions that would later support American
nationalism and democratic culture. Although older ideas and values
guided the first abolitionists, such as Granville Sharp and Olaudah
Equiano, these newer notions would ultimately inform nineteenth-century abolitionism and the free Black communities of North America. In
political thought, the sovereignty of Parliament and the justice of virtual
representation lost their power in America as republican notions of gov-
ernance and citizenship attracted the patriots of the Revolutionary era.
Federalist views of a strong national government prevailed at the
Philadelphia convention and in the ratification in most of the states,
giving Americans, with significant modifications insisted upon by the
Antifederalists, their Constitution. Yet both republican ideology and
the Federalist Party of George Washington, John Adams, and
Alexander Hamilton were overwhelmed by democratic culture by 1830,
allowing a new form of abolitionism to replace the eighteenth-century

version. In philosophy, faith both in human reason, including the ability to comprehend the divine will, and in human sociability worked against older views that reason functioned well only in a small sphere, that God's will was ultimately inscrutable, and that ordinary people required moral authority imposed from above by church or state to circumvent their falling into a war of all against all. In Protestantism, Calvinist theology was challenged not only by free-will religion but also by the proliferation of new Christian sects and denominations claiming distinctive revelations. Long-standing prejudices against Islam were sharpened as it became seen as a foil to the religion of a free society. And some vocal Americans and Britons, both Black and white, began to agitate against the Atlantic slave trade and slavery. Quick on the heels of those protests was a debate about the likelihood of integrating former slaves into a free society—a debate in which one side promoted the expatriation of free Blacks, "colonized" in the West Indies or West Africa. Politics, philosophy, religion, and animus against Islam all became wrapped up in the debate about slavery and the future of former slaves. The modern Anglophone nations of Sierra Leone and Liberia were founded in these years, the former with little expatriationist urgency but the latter out of a drive to rid North America of free Blacks.[1]

124

These decades were also the formative period of African-American literature. In colonial, revolutionary, national, and transatlantic contexts, Black men and Black women wrote and published. Their words appeared as poems, hymns, prayers, journals, autobiographies, sermons, petitions, travelogues, histories, commentaries on theology, and manifestos on politics, slavery, and colonization. This chapter is both a reflection on instructing students in the content and value of these African-American texts and a commentary on the some of the challenges of doing so well in the early twenty-first century.[2]

Slaves and Free blacks alike were denied virtually all the benefits of citizenship. The very definition of a slave was a noncitizen. Yet some African-American men had worn the badge of citizenship—virtuous service in the War of Independence. The preoccupation of many early African-American writings became the quest for citizenship, incited and enacted first in the revolutionary fervor. This is both valuable and challenging in our own time because citizenship itself, at least as a portion of the American population understands it, is under attack. Americans of the revolutionary era would have recognized one of the tenacious and long-lived foes of citizenship: an excess of self-concern that turns one too far away from the public sphere. But in our time an abandonment of the public dimension of life—the refusal of a citizen's life—has paradoxically become a virtue. Not only privacy but also hostility to the public sphere is celebrated in American political culture. Furthermore, in the early twenty-first century, as if through a glass darkly to those who hold in mind the constitution writing of the revolutionary era, some Americans are turning to amendments of state constitutions, ratified by popular vote, as a way to limit rights as well as to deny other Americans the opportunity to argue for their rights in courts of law. Even if we recognize that some of the state constitutions contained limitations we would not accept today (such as religious qualifications for officeholders) we may well think that our nation is misusing the constitutional tradition. Indeed, it seems a dark time for those whose rights are not supported by a politically active majority. It is at this very time in our national history that we should be returning to the formative documents of our revolutionary period—concerned as it was with citizenship—as well as to African-American writing ranging from the late colonial years to the early republic.

Current tools for teaching African-American literature in survey courses are ill suited for engaging the issue of citizenship. Anthologies such as *The Norton Anthology of African American Literature* situate early African-American writing in folkloric and West African contexts in which citizenship could be only an alien idea. The most profound engagement we might find with such contexts in mind is ironic commentary, sometimes called signifying, on citizenship. But such commentary was rare in early Black writing, whose authors were ironic not about citizenship or Christianity, but about citizens and Christians who set themselves against enslaved Blacks. Early Black writers used elements of those folkloric and West African contexts—and at that, only infrequently—in making their arguments about citizenship. A distorted view arises when we mistake one element in an argument for its foundation. Moreover, our political culture falters when we cannot rely on it to help us understand the American Revolution and its aftermath.

Ironically, some dispossessed Blacks of late-eighteenth-century and early-nineteenth-century America had a clearer understanding of the founding of the new nation than many in our time who have not only the opportunity but also the responsibility to know better.

Republican thought guided the revolutionary activities of the patriots. The colonists situated a well-established English language of rights in a republican context constructed from ancient, Christian, and modern elements. Republicans feared and fought against slavery as defined by eighteenth-century British thought—the tyranny of rulers. It was a citizen's act, it was virtue enacted, to resist tyranny. At least some whites, loyalists and patriots alike, saw the enslavement of Blacks as tyrannical in the same way, as the despotism of masters and legislatures over Blacks. The same perception stirred Black commentary. The love of liberty notwithstanding, republican thought concerned itself with the centripetal force of society, the way in which it would cohere over time and space without the authority of kings and aristocrats. This

unifying force were the social affections, the benevolence, sensibility, and sentiment that adherents of both Christianity and the Enlightenment saw at work in society. The social affections were the necessary condition of virtue, not a classical, martial self-denial but a modern devotion to the life and liberty of one's compatriots. The first Anglo-American criticisms of the slave trade and slavery had at least as much to do with masters' violations of virtue and the social affections as with the loss of liberty. Some of the early white abolitionists perceived these violations from a distance, but all the early Black abolitionists understood firsthand the cost of the slave system to social morality. Rights, tyranny, slavery, liberty, affection, virtue: together these were a clarion call to Black authors.[3]

For instance, Lemuel Haynes used these republican notions of liberty and social cohesion against the slave trade and slavery beginning in the 1770s. His wartime protests against the slave trade and slavery were followed in the next few decades by commentary on the affections and the virtue that Blacks and whites could share. For Haynes, freedom, affection, and virtue were the steps leading to citizenship.[4] Assuming that Blacks and whites could live united in virtue, Phillis Wheatley envisioned both the acceptance of Blacks and a free society following a patriot victory. Here, in lines from several poems, she cast a Black person as virtuous, she insisted on the spiritual equality of the races, and she prophesied American freedom:

> But, O my soul, sink not into despair,
> *Virtue* is near thee, and with gentle hand
> Would now embrace thee, hovers o'er thine head.
> ("On VIRTUE")
> . . . .
> Remember, *Christians*, *Negros*, black as *Cain*,
> May be refin'd, and join th' angelic train.
> ("On being brought from AFRICA to AMERICA")
> . . . .
> Auspicious Heaven shall fill with fav'ring Gales,
> Where e'er *Columbia* spreads her swelling Sails:
> To every Realm shall *Peace* her Charms display,
> And Heavenly *Freedom* spreads her golden Ray.
> ("Liberty and Peace")[5]

127

Wheatley would never have been bold enough to demand a masculine role in her society, but she envisioned a society of Blacks and whites coexisting, and she embodied literary culture herself as well as praising artistic talent in other Blacks. As Phillip M. Richards has noted, Wheatley's patriotism was worked together with her literary use of her African origins.[6] Richard Allen and Absalom Jones castigated white Philadelphians for their lack of affection and benevolence when faced with the virtue of Blacks who were serving their city during the yellow fever epidemic.[7] Prince Hall complained about the danger to Black Bostonians going about their ordinary business on city streets.[8]

Calvinism influenced this generation of Black writers, blending with the republican cause as it did for many of their white contemporaries. The social ethic of late-eighteenth-century Calvinism sometimes fortified the impulse to integrate Blacks as citizens, yet Calvinists, both Black and white, could be among the most intransigent of the separatists. For instance, white Calvinists were often pessimistic about future relations with Blacks, while a predestinarian utopianism seems to have motivated the Black Huntingdonian minister John Marrant to urge a holy remnant of Blacks to sail from North America to Sierra Leone.[9]

For Black writers of the late eighteenth century and early nineteenth century, citizenship sometimes meant the franchise, liberty, and property rights, but it also meant the recognition of Blacks' value in society. Black men and Black women wanted recognition and respect for their contributions to society. Some contributions were literary, as with Wheatley. Some were religious, as with Allen and Haynes. Some were martial, as with Haynes and the Black soldiers of the War of Independence. Some were commercial, as with Olaudah Equiano and the petty commerce he engaged in as a slave and, later, the significant profit he made as a freedman from sales of his autobiography. Some were political, as with Equiano's and Ottobah Cugoano's agitation against the slave trade.

Anthologies of African-American literature omit one of the forms of writing most often used by Black men and Black women before the middle of the nineteenth century: a political form, the petition. Petitions should be an essential text in an anthology: they were written by politically active Blacks, but usually not by the well-known luminaries, and their language is among the closest records of the Black vernacular of the times, since their authors were often semiliterate and the manuscripts that exist are often not polished copies but rather texts with corrections in the author's hand. Yet they are absent from anthologies, while transcriptions of folktales, which are almost certainly quite distant from what was the language of ordinary Blacks, are present in numbers.

In the Anglo-American tradition, petitions were one of the most revered expressions of citizenship—an exercise of a political right dating to medieval times—so it makes sense that in a time of enervated citizenship the history of petitions is little appreciated. Petitions were well known to African-Americans of the revolutionary era and the early republic. Black men and a few Black women used petitions to request wages, freedom, or loans or to protest generally against slavery. Indeed, in reading their petitions we trace the creation of abolitionism, for the documents move from objections to particular wrongs done individual slaves to protests against the institution of slavery itself. In 1797, when abolitionism had coalesced on both sides of the Atlantic, four Black men petitioned the Connecticut state legislature on behalf of "a very numerous class of men of their own colour, who are holden in bondage." Words in square brackets were crossed out by the authors or are my comments on illegibility or lack of clarity; words in angle brackets were added by the authors as superscript:

That the petitioners are inhabitants of this State subject to the Laws & [subject] <entitled> to the privileges & immunities of the other inhabitants. They conceive that the Laws of Nature & even the Declaration of the rights of the people of this State when taken in its true Spirit, declare that they are entitled to the same freedom & to the common privileges of their fellow men. That all men are born entitled to equal freedom & to equal protection from the laws of their Country. . . . Your Petitioners having been trained up in Slavery deprived of any instruction but to obey, untaught almost the first principles of Religion, are sensible of the disadvantages under which they labour & ever must labour while Slaves in attempting to assume a place in the ranks of Freemen: but when encouraged by the profession of Liberty & educated in the same manner & with the same prospect of advantage with the other Inhabitants of the State, they hope to prove themselves equally quite Subjects of Government & equally useful members of Society—But at present, without any clear explicit law to warrant, your petitioners are holden in bondage, are restrained in their persons, have their Goods & Estate taken away, are liable to be deprived of their wives & children, or to be sold into bondage where the rigours of slavery cannot be softened by the Society of their Families. Your Petitioners will ever feel grateful for the <partial> emancipation [of] <which has been extended to> many of their colour & are encouraged by it to pray that this Honourable Assembly [illegible words crossed out] <by> a General Act [illegible words crossed out] to free from the bonds of Slavery those Negroes in this State, who are yet holden in bondage & your Petitioners as in duty bound will ever pray. Dated at Hartford this 18th day of May AD 1797

Caesar Augustus Robinson[?]
James Cromwell
Freeman Augustus Hills
John Barter[10]

It was significant that Blacks used one of the most venerated rights in the Anglo-American tradition when they petitioned legislatures and public officials. It was an act that revealed their struggles to exist as citizens even when their society denied their desires; it was also a bridge to the white patriots of the revolution. Thomas Jefferson's *Summary View of the Rights of British America* originated as a petition. George III's refusal to hear petitions from Americans infuriated the colonists, and Thomas Paine identified this as a major grievance of the 1770s. And among the first petitions submitted to the federal Congress after the ratification of the Constitution was one advocating regulation and limitation of the Atlantic slave trade.

When Black men petitioned, they were exercising their rights and expressing their sense of citizenship—not ironically but insistently and prospectively. They were also articulating a belief that is at best now subterranean in our political culture: that citizens are, in the words of the Connecticut Blacks, "duty bound" to request that their rights be protected by the state and recognized in law. The government should protect human rights not only from infringement by its laws but also from the will of the powerful or of the majority. This 1797 petition rested on thirty years of American thought about republican citizenship, constitutionalism, and rights. Only conversance with American founding ideas and values allows one to understand this.

Another work that can be hardly appreciated in our political climate is David Walker's *Appeal*.[11] As presented in anthologies, the *Appeal* appears as an expression of Black oral culture and a link between earlier slave resistance and antebellum abolitionism.[12] The text itself does seem to be a transcription of Black speech at least in style if not in diction. And Peter Hinks, the leading scholar on Walker, has theorized that he was influenced by the Denmark Vesey case, and in any event Walker himself does recommend insurrection.[13] However, the *Appeal* exhibits a sophisticated use of the texts of the revolutionary era beyond the ones Walker named such as the Declaration of Independence and Jefferson's *Notes on the State of Virginia*. Indeed, Walker seems to have named white authors when he disagreed with them—Jefferson the most obvious— but not when he agreed with them. This strategy fit in with his call for Black independence. Moreover, Walker was known in his lifetime for his devotion to reading. William Lloyd Garrison wrote, for instance, "We are assured, by those who intimately knew him, that his *Appeal* was an exact transcript of his daily conversations; that, within the last four years, he was hurtfully indefatigable in his studies."[14] The *Appeal* is profoundly intertextual, and Walker almost certainly relied on Thomas Paine's *Common Sense, The American Crisis, The Rights of Man,* and *The Age of Reason* as well as Publius's *The Federalist.* All these works were easily available in Boston in the 1820s. The radicalism of the *Appeal* derives as much from its use of these American documents as from its opposition to slavery. Walker was attracted by writings that urged resistance and a mental revolution among the harassed and oppressed as well as by writings that promoted liberty and security in the postrevolutionary period, whether this was after the War of Independence, after the liberation of Black slaves, or after Blacks' self-liberation from the chains of racism.

In the brief catalog that follows, some of Walker's borrowings are listed. The travels Walker described in the first sentence of the *Appeal,* "over a considerable portion of these United States," were more likely to have been in books than in the nation. As Hinks has noted, there is in fact no evidence of Walker's travels.[15] Walker wrote, "Having travelled over a considerable portion of these United States, and having, in the course of my travels, taken the most accurate observation of things as they exist—the result of my observations has warranted the full and unshaken conviction, that we, (coloured people of these United States), are the most degraded, wretched, and abject set of beings that ever lived since the world began."[16] This first sentence sets a pattern repeated throughout the *Appeal:* Walker knew "things as they exist" from books as well as from experience. He knew the language of revolutionary America and he used it not only in his work but also to structure his work. "The result of my observations" mirrors phrases in *The Federalist* 16, 36, and 84. "Since the world began" is a phrase that appears in Paine's *American Crisis,* as is "to the satisfaction of the most incredulous mind," which Walker used in the first sentence in the next paragraph.[17]

Here is a catalog of some of the other borrowings, all of which appear just in the "Preamble" and "Article I" of the *Appeal.* The catalog would be longer were the other articles considered. Indeed, the words

Preamble and *Article* are prominent in the United States Constitution itself. Even the first part of the title, *David Walker's Appeal*, may have been inspired by Paine's comments, in *Rights of Man*, on Edmund Burke's *Appeal* ("Mr. Burke's 'Appeal.' ").[18] I have limited myself to quotations, except for a few near-quotations all indicated by parenthesis; a looser standard, marking paraphrases, reveals even more instances. Each quotation appeared in the *Appeal*, followed by titles by Paine or Publius in which the same words were used at least once. While Walker seems to have quoted some of the following words and phrases, the more general point is that the shared diction of Walker, Paine, and Publius was not typical of other Black-authored texts before 1830. Walker's diction indicates concerns and structures of thought common to the *Appeal* and Paine's and Publius's writings. Accordingly, I have omitted words that were so common, such as *duty*, that Walker could have absorbed them from conversation or casual reading, even though they appear in all the texts under consideration. Yet I have included seemingly casual or off-hand phrases such as *I am persuaded* not because they are unique to the texts under consideration but because they are part of a pattern of borrowings and, indeed, structures of thought.

132

"Reflecting mind": *Age of Reason.*[19]

"I am persuaded": *American Crisis.*[20]

"Ignorant": *American Crisis, Age of Reason,* and *The Federalist* 53 and 57.[21]

"A spirit of inquiry": *The Rights of Man* ("a spirit of political inquiry").[22]

"Land of Liberty": *American Crisis.*[23]

"Expose them": *American Crisis.*[24]

"Learn wisdom": *Common Sense.*[25]

"Usurpers": *Rights of Man* and *The Federalist* 18, 28, 29, and 41.[26]

"Sword in hand": *The Federalist* 84.[27]

"In consequence of": *Age of Reason,* and *The Federalist* 7, 26, and 32.[28]

"Unprejudiced": *The Federalist* 23.[29]

"Acquainted with history": *Age of Reason* ("acquainted with ecclesiastical history").[30]

"Actuated": *The Federalist* 1, 10, 15, 29, 60, and 64.[31]

"View . . . things as they were": *American Crisis* ("things be viewed as they really were").[32]

"Dispense with": *The Federalist* 26 and 29.[33]

"Procrastinated": *The Federalist* 65.[34]

"Impunity": *The Federalist* 27, 43, 66, 69, and 74.[35]

"Subjected": *Common Sense, American Crisis* and *The Federalist* 7, 8, 12, 22, 25, 30, 43, 69, and 77.[36]

"Ought to be free": Declaration of Independence and *The Federalist* 84 (footnote, by Publius).[37]

"The minds of all unprejudiced men": *The Federalist* 23 ("a correct and unprejudiced mind").[38]

"Need no elucidation": *The Federalist* 11 ("does not require a particular elucidation").[39]

"I appeal": *The Federalist* 41.[40]

"Great Republic": *Rights of Man.*[41]

"Pass . . . in review": *The Federalist* 24.[42]

"Notorious fact": *The Federalist* 83.[43]

"Vested": *The Federalist* 3, 19, 23, 24, 33, 36, 39, 40, 41, 44, 45, 47, 52, 62, 69, 73, 76, 77, 81, 82, 83 (footnote, by Publius), and 84.[44]

"Suffered to remain": *American Crisis* ("suffer . . . to remain").[45]

"This the case": *Rights of Man.*[46]

"Readily admit": *American Crisis* and *The Federalist* 35.[47]

"History, either sacred or profane": *The Federalist* 33 ("nor sacred nor profane").[48]

"Deplorable condition": *Rights of Man.*[49]

"Insupportable": *The Federalist* 22.[50]

"To contend for": *The Federalist* 58.[51]

"I cannot conceive": *Age of Reason* ("we cannot conceive").[52]

"World knows": *Rights of Man.*[53]

"A cypher": *Rights of Man.*[54]

"Very learned": *Age of Reason.*[55]

"With avidity": *The Federalist* 7.[56]

"Refutations": *The Federalist* 83 and 85 (total of three instances, all singular).[57]

"In consequence of": *American Crisis, Rights of Man,* and *The Federalist* 7, 26, and 32.[58]

"Govern ourselves": *American Crisis.*[59]

"Much mistaken": *The Federalist* 26.[60]

"Greatest object": *The Federalist* 2, 10, 11, 40, 83 ("great object" and variations).[61]

"To a close": *Rights of Man* and *Age of Reason*.[62]

"Dust" and "dying worms": *Common Sense* (latter singular).[63]

"What right": *Rights of Man*.[64]

"Shut up": *American Crisis, Rights of Man, Age of Reason,* and *The Federalist* 77.[65]

"Power and authority": *American Crisis* and *The Federalist* 23, 33, 34, 78, 82 (used together numerous times but not with only one conjunction or other intervening word).[66]

"We view": *American Crisis, Common Sense,* and *Rights of Man*.[67]

"Accountable": *American Crisis* and *The Federalist* 55.[68]

"Deceitful": *Rights of Man* and *The Federalist* 6.[69]

"Positively a fact": *American Crisis* ("positive fact").[70]

"Prejudice": *Common Sense, Age of Reason,* and *The Federalist* 8, 12, 14, 15, 31, 35, 43, 60, 63, 76, 84, and 85.[71]

Some clustering of the quotations and paraphrases suggests that Walker had particular interest or perhaps time to read especially carefully in certain numbers and runs of *The Federalist:* 7–12, 23–35, 40–43, 69, 73–78, and 83–85. And this repetition of words and phrases from Paine's and Publius's writings continued in the other articles of the *Appeal.*

Some of these words and phrases were commonplaces of eighteenth-century diction, but many of them almost certainly passed into the *Appeal* from Walker's reading of Paine and Publius. He may have also been aware of other writings by two of the Publius contributors (Alexander Hamilton and James Madison) as well as of Antifederalist critiques of the results of the federal convention, but the repetition of words and phrases from Paine's writings and *The Federalist* is so consistent throughout the *Appeal* and so constitutive of it that a good part of its sources are identifiable. Many teachers and scholars of African-American literature will mentally reinsert most of these words and phrases into Walker's preamble and first article, which are the most commonly anthologized parts of the *Appeal.* Unfortunately, few will do the same with Paine's writings or *The Federalist.* Thus we miss the genesis and the significance of the *Appeal.*

Walker was almost certainly drawing on three important strands in revolutionary thought: a radicalism protective of rights, a demand for individual responsibility in a revolutionary situation, and the need for postrevolutionary structures that will preserve rights. Of course, the end of slavery was a revolution for African-Americans. Paine's and Publius's general concerns became racially specific in the *Appeal*: the implementation of Blacks' rights, a responsibility shouldered by Blacks themselves, and the protection of rights through the mentality and forms of African-American society. Paine was among the most insistent of eighteenth-century writers that government respect individual rights, and in a late publication, *Agrarian Justice*, he argued that governments should compensate the lowly and the dispossessed for the loss of the rights in social property they had suffered. Individual responsibility was one of the pleas of *The American Crisis*. *The Federalist* is, of course, often thought of as a defense of an energetic and powerful national government, but one of Publius's purposes was the preservation of American republicanism. James Madison may have resisted the addition of a list of rights to the Constitution, but he did at last compose the amendments that became the American Bill of Rights. Walker as well as Paine and Publius asked how liberty can be saved from those, both Black and white, who would undermine it. One of the most powerful thrusts of the *Appeal* was the argument that some African-Americans themselves were working against the liberty of all Blacks: *The Federalist* had made the same point about whites at large and the freedom of all Americans. Both *The Federalist* and the *Appeal* demanded action against the forces that threaten freedom. Both postrevolutionary and postslavery times demanded reliable structures in thought and society to preserve freedom in the face of forces that would cripple it. Put simply, Walker absorbed from Paine the necessity of a mental revolution (for Blacks) and from Publius the importance of ideas and institutions that would work against the ill effects of factionalism (among Blacks). We can even go further and note that the structuring principles of the *Appeal*—not just what it says but what guides what it says—derive from the American Revolution and its texts.

Since Paine seems to have been prominent in Walker's reading, it is worth thinking about Walker's attraction to *Common Sense, The American Crisis, The Rights of Man,* and *The Age of Reason.* Surely Walker noted

Paine's sentence in *Common Sense*, "When Republican virtue fails, slavery ensues." *Common Sense* meant to mobilize Americans for revolution, and *The American Crisis* meant to sustain the patriots' spirits and souls in the depths of the war and to insist on their responsibility (as well as that of the British commanders) in the War of Independence. *The Rights of Man* sought to reconstitute Paine's audience into a more republican body. Walker's *Appeal* transferred these intentions to his own audience. Pauline Maier's description of the effect of *Common Sense* sounds like what Walker hoped the *Appeal* would work among African-Americans. Both texts urged an end to accommodation and a rebellion against the oppressors and the indifferent:

> The most important single restraint on any decision for independence, however, was the hope that somehow, whether by action of the ministry, Parliament, King, or the British people, an accommodation within the framework of the empire might yet be made between the colonists and Britain, with "the terms and limits of our union" ascertained and fixed "upon clear and solid ground." This hope lingered on into late 1775; but with the failure of the English people to rise in support of the Americans it was extinguished, and independence became imperative. It was at that time that Thomas Paine published *Common Sense*. The pamphlet was credited with converting many, particularly in the South, to independence.[72]

In the twenty years after the publication of *Common Sense* and *The American Crisis*, Paine turned his attention, with *The Rights of Man* and *The Age of Reason*, to stirring a mental revolution in his audience—which was the essential task of Walker's *Appeal*.

Paine's *Rights of Man* was meant to convert and reform his readers, as he implied in the introduction to part 2 in writing, "What Archimedes said of the mechanical powers, may be applied to Reason and Liberty. 'Had we,' said he 'a place to stand upon, we might raise the world.'" In a sentence that Walker echoed, Paine wrote, "Independence is my happiness, and I view things as they are, without regard to place or person; my country is the world, and my religion to do good." *The Age of Reason* followed Paine's earlier works in attempting to demonstrate the mental and moral states that suited the independence and benevolence of citizens—once again an apt description of some of the purposes of the *Appeal.*

Walker advocated a mental revolution among Blacks along with practices and forms in African-American society that would fortify its liberty. He scorned the deference, the cowardice, and the selfishness among Blacks that put them in some way in league with slave traders and slaveholders. The parallel with the American Revolution and the late 1780s is clear, but what has not been recognized is that Walker relied on the documents of the 1770s and 1780s for the *Appeal.* The structures of thought represented in Walker's prose derive from the revolutionary era, while the content is African-American. In the early twenty-first century, our scholarship and our anthologies hardly allow us to appreciate Walker. Indeed, they tend to remove him from his base in revolutionary ideas and values and situate him solely in African and African-American contexts, inevitably creating only a partial view of a crucial Black writer. A full view is all the more needed in our times, since so much of the Revolution is now lost to us.

137

Notes

1. Stephen J. Braidwood, *Black Poor and White Philanthropists: London's Blacks and the Foundation of the Sierra Leone Settlement 1786–1791* (Liverpool: Liverpool University Press, 1994), 129–79, argues that the migration of Blacks from England to Sierra Leone was not a deportation. Two articles touching on the coercion implicit in American colonization schemes, which came to fruition in Liberia in the early 1820s, are John Saillant, "Lemuel Haynes's Black Republicanism and the American Republican Tradition, 1775–1820," *Journal of the Early Republic* 14, no. 3 (fall 1994): 293–324, and John Saillant, "The American Enlightenment in Africa: Jefferson's Colonizationism and Black Virginians' Migration to Liberia, 1776–1840," *Eighteenth-Century Studies* 31, no. 3 (spring 1998): 261–82.

2. Two recent collections, both of which seek a high standard in transcription and annotation, despite the inevitable disagreements among scholars, are *Unchained Voices: An Anthology of Black Authors in the English-Speaking World of the Eighteenth Century*, ed. Vincent Carretta (Lexington: University Press of Kentucky, 1996), and *"Face Zion Forward": First Writers of the Black Atlantic*, ed. Joanna Brooks and John Saillant (Boston: Northeastern University Press, 2002). Readers can easily compare these collections to a popular anthology such as *The Norton Anthology of African American Literature*, 2d ed., ed. Henry Louis Gates Jr. et al., which categorizes early writings within "The Literature of Slavery and Freedom, 1746–1865," (151–540) and situates them after "The Vernacular Tradition" (3–149).

3. A recent synopsis of the complexities of revolutionary republicanism is Gordon S. Wood, *The American Revolution: A History* (New York: The Modern Library, 2002), esp. 91–135.

4. John Saillant, *Black Puritan, Black Republican: The Life and Thought of Lemuel Haynes, 1753–1833* (New York: Oxford University Press, 2003).

5. *The Collected Works of Phillis Wheatley*, ed. John Shields (New York: Oxford University Press, 1988), 13, 18, 155–56.

6. Phillip M. Richards, "Phillis Wheatley and Literary Americanization," *American Quarterly* 44 (1992): 163–91.

7. Richard Allen, *The Life Experience and Gospel Labors of the Rt. Rev. Richard Allen, To Which Is Annexed The Rise and Progress of the African Methodist Episcopal Church in the United States of America, Containing a Narrative of the Yellow Fever in the Year of Our Lord 1793, With an Address to the People of Color in the United States, Written by Himself and Published at His Request* (New York: Abingdon Press, 1969).

8. Prince Hall, *A Charge, Delivered to the African Lodge June 24, 1797 at Metonomy*, in *"Face Zion Forward,"* 198–208, esp. 203–4.

9. Saillant, *Black Puritan, Black Republican*, 83–116. John Saillant, " 'Wipe Away All Tears from Their Eyes': John Marrant's Theology in the Black Atlantic, 1785–1808," *Journal of Millennial Studies* 1, no. 2 (winter 1999); http://www.mille.org/jrnlwin99.htm. Joanna Brooks, *American Lazarus: Religion and the Rise of African-American and Native American Literatures* (New York: Oxford University Press, 2003), 87–113.

10. Document held at the Connecticut State Archives, Hartford.

11. The standard edition of the *Appeal* is David Walker's *Appeal to the Coloured Citizens of the World*, ed. Peter P. Hinks (University Park: Pennsylvania State University Press, 2000).

12. This is also the argument of Peter P. Hinks, *To Awaken My Afflicted Brethren: David Walker and the Problem of Antebellum Slave Resistance* (University Park: Pennsylvania State University Press, 1997). See, for instance, 46–62 and p. 193, where Hinks writes, "Walker's *Appeal* had its roots in an oral, not a print, culture."

13. Hinks, *To Awaken My Afflicted Brethren*, 30–40.

14. *The Liberator*, January 29, 1831, quoted in Hinks, *To Awaken My Afflicted Brethren*, 117.

15. Hinks, *To Awaken My Afflicted Brethren*, 64–65.

16. *Appeal*, 3.

17. *Appeal*, 3; Thomas Paine, *The American Crisis*, in *The Writings of Thomas Paine*, ed. Moncure Daniel Conway (New York: G. P. Putman's Sons, 1894), 1:249; *The Federalist*, ed. Jacob E. Cooke (Middletown, CT: Wesleyan University Press, 1961), 102, 222, 587.

18. *Rights of Man*, 395.

19. *Appeal*, 4; *The Age of Reason*, 4:189.

20. *Appeal*, 4; *American Crisis*, 251, 284 (two times).

21. *Appeal*, 4; *American Crisis*, 195, 206, 250, 263, 265; *Age of Reason*, 124, 130; *The Federalist*, 365, 385.

22. *Appeal*, 5; *The Rights of Man*, 2:334.

23. *Appeal*, 5; *American Crisis*, 367.

24. *Appeal*, 5; *American Crisis*, 223.

25. *Appeal*, 5; *Common Sense*, 1:108.

26. *Appeal*, 5 (two times); *Rights of Man*, 277; *The Federalist*, 118, 178–79 (three times), 186, 305.

27. *Appeal*, 5; *The Federalist*, 578.

28. *Appeal*, 6; *Age of Reason*, 71, 94, 112 132, 135; *The Federalist*, 42, 170, 200.

29. *Appeal*, 6; *The Federalist*, 147.

30. *Appeal*, 6; *Age of Reason*, 170.

31. *Appeal*, 6; *The Federalist*, 4, 57, 96, 187, 402, 435.

32. *Appeal*, 7; *American Crisis*, 253.

33. *Appeal*, 7; *The Federalist*, 170, 182.

34. *Appeal*, 7; *The Federalist*, 444.

35. *Appeal*, 7; *The Federalist*, 173, 289, 451, 466, 502–3.

36. *Appeal*, 9, 15; *Common Sense*, 81; *American Crisis*, 351, 358; *The Federalist*, 27, 48, 79, 142, 158, 188, 297, 463, 530.

37. *Appeal*, 9; *The Federalist*, 580.

38. *Appeal*, 9; *The Federalist*, 147.

39. *Appeal*, 9; *The Federalist*, 71.

40. *Appeal*, 10; *The Federalist*, 278.

41. *Appeal*, 10; *Rights of Man*, 453.

42. *Appeal*, 10, 11; *The Federalist*, 153.

43. *Appeal*, 11; *The Federalist*, 574.

44. *Appeal*, 11; *The Federalist*, 13, 118, 152, 204, 227, 229, 256, 266, 268, 302, 305, 311, 314, 330, 358, 415, 462, 465, 494, 497, 498, 510, 517, 542, 554, 557, 573, 579.

45. *Appeal*, 12; *American Crisis*, 303.

46. *Appeal*, 12; *Rights of Man*, 318, 387.

47. *Appeal*, 12; *American Crisis*, 234; *The Federalist*, 218.

48. *Appeal*, 12; *The Federalist*, 204.

49. *Appeal*, 12; *Rights of Man*, 488.

50. *Appeal*, 12; *The Federalist*, 137.

51. *Appeal*, 14; *The Federalist*, 394.

52. *Appeal*, 16.

53. *Appeal*, 16; *Rights of Man*, 396.

54. *Appeal*, 16; *Rights of Man*, 373.

55. *Appeal*, 16.

56. *Appeal*, 16; *The Federalist*, 42.

57. *Appeal*, 17; *The Federalist*, 558, 561, 589.

58. *Appeal*, 17; *American Crisis*, 256; *The Federalist*, 42, 170, 200.

59. *Appeal*, 17; *American Crisis*, 252.

60. *Appeal*, 18; *The Federalist*, 165.

61. *Appeal*, 18; *The Federalist*, 12, 61, 70, 264, 572.

62. *Appeal*, 18; *Rights of Man*, 394.

63. *Appeal*, 18; *Common Sense*, 76, 113.

64. *Appeal*, 18; *Rights of Man*, 415, 468.

65. *Appeal*, 19; *American Crisis*, 256, 318, 319; *Rights of Man*, 291, 342–43; *The Federalist*, 517.

66. *Appeal*, 19; *American Crisis*, 190, 257; *The Federalist*, 149, 208, 214, 524, 554.

67. *Appeal*, 19 (three times); *Common Sense* (appendix), 122; *American Crisis*, 380; *Rights of Man*, 322, 327.

68. *Appeal*, 19; *American Crisis*, 292, 358; *The Federalist*, 377.

69. *Appeal*, 19; *Rights of Man*, 512; *The Federalist*, 34.

70. *Appeal*, 19; *American Crisis*, 315.

71. *Appeal*, 19; *Common Sense*, 71, 74, 75, 84, 87, 105; *The Federalist*, 48, 76, 83, 91, 194, 221, 291, 404, 425, 513, 583, 590.

72. Pauline Maier, *From Resistance to Revolution: Colonial Radicals and the Development of American Opposition to Britain, 1765–1776* (New York: Alfred A. Knopf, 1972), 267.

Xiomara Santamarina

$\mathcal{A}$ntebellum African-American Texts beyond Slavery and Race

STUDENTS OF NINETEENTH-CENTURY AMERICAN LITERATURE are often quite surprised to discover that free African-Americans, and even some former slaves, did not see the abolition of slavery as the only topic worth writing and publishing about. In the course that I teach at the University of Michigan, I complicate the conversation about race and literature by offering students a wide selection of texts that sparks their interest in the texts and issues of a Black community far more heterogeneous than slave narratives and abolitionist discourse often lead them to expect. These texts often do not fit our notions of racial literature and protest and include slave narratives that were not sanctioned by abolitionists: books by free Black workers that do not feature the fight against slavery, novels, travel narratives, and protosociological texts by freeborn Blacks that speak to the diverse experiences and concerns of nineteenth-century Black communities across the nation. (I retain the "antebellum" periodization notwithstanding its association with slavery and abolition since my effort moves "beyond" abolition but retains the importance of the pre– and post–Civil War periods in shaping African-American and American print contexts.) I encourage students to read a range of genres with an eye to discovering "multiple" African-American literary traditions and the various discursive strategies Black authors employed to appeal to "multiple" publics, North, South, and West.

Since many of my students will have little familiarity with Black literature beyond Douglass's 1845 narrative, the notion of "multiple traditions" as opposed to a "tradition" is potentially too abstract a framework for them. For this reason, I organize the course by genre and I pair what I term the *traditional* text that represents that genre with other texts that refer to different discursive contexts or have different discursive goals. I have found that this is a good approach to having it both ways, so to speak; it acquaints students with the abolition- and slavery-centered African-American texts and contexts in tandem with, even if sometimes in opposition to, texts and contexts that discuss race in other more nuanced and atypical ways. Most importantly, it exposes students to the reality that Black writers conceived the literature of racial "protest" and literary forms in very diverse ways and that the category of "race" itself does not appear as self-evident as we might assume. This makes more sense to students than one might expect because it foregrounds a very basic contradiction: while they often desire to romanticize a text's racial content (or its author's racial identity), they also realize, contra Langston Hughes, that the "racial mountain" he urged Black authors to tackle can really be a burden that reproduces rather than counteracts the asymmetrical representational field that Black authors and artists inhabit.[1] I encourage students to explore this gap between the protest imperative to romanticize Black writers' texts and students' own nuanced recognition that it is unfair for modern readers to demand certain literary forms, like realism or slave narratives, from writers, simply because they are Black. This approach opens up for consideration the various and often contradictory ways in which "race" makes an appearance in African-Americans' texts and intersects and converges with other relevant formations like class, region, and gender. Fortunately, I find that more students today (even if not all) are willing to embrace the notion of heterogeneous communities of Black writers and readers than they were five years to a decade ago, when anything that did not fit their narrow notion of race literature a la *Native Son, Invisible Man,* or *Beloved* was derided as accommodationist, or even "white."

We start with autobiography and with the Ur-text itself, Douglass's 1845 *Narrative,* to foreground the different kinds of autobiography that were central to the emergence of African-American writing from the period. (When I teach a course on the slave narrative, the 1845 narrative is introduced midway in the semester and makes for a very interesting change of pace.) When we read the *Narrative* I pair it with an excerpt from William Andrews's essay on Frederick Douglass's discussion of the North to encourage students to recognize how daring *and* politically savvy Douglass was as narrator and famous former slave.[2] I find it is very important to make it clear from the start that this compelling and seemingly seamless narrative responds very systematically to the assumptions and biases of a northern white audience from a particular period. By selecting specific episodes—the one recounting his separation from his mother, or his learning to read, for example—we work together to see the audience assumptions that Douglass attempts to counter. In this way the narrative offers an opportunity quickly to set the abolitionist stage for students who might be unfamiliar with the nineteenth century in general. Ideally we discuss how rhetorical persuasion was a key goal, rather than any kind of a "sell-out," yet we also discuss how as modern readers we still find the American individualist ideal dramatized in Douglass's text a compelling, if romantic, one. The narrative exemplifies what I address as a key dynamic of these texts, one of "constraints and opportunities;" a dynamic that exploits the rhetorical possibilities that abolitionist discourse offered, while also dramatizing its constraints. The brief secondary reading I assign helps students see how Douglass's audience influenced what he chose to tell and what he chose to hide (in particular, about the North) in a text that reads like a daring tell-all. When we make Douglass's audience "visible" in this way, students are more willing to consider the compromises and choices that Black writers made in a more historically informed and sensitive way. (For the most part, I provide students with a sense of these texts' audiences and print contexts through "minilectures.")

Even as we recognize the centrality of autobiography to African-American literary traditions, the remaining autobiographical texts in the course are ones that are not typically taught in African-American literature courses. One written by another former slave, *Life of William Grimes, the Runaway Slave, Written by Himself* (1825; 1855), was conspicuously ignored by abolitionists; the other, *The Memoirs of Elleanor Eldridge* (1838), is a biography about an entrepreneurial free woman from Rhode Island, Elleanor Eldridge. The *Memoirs* was written by an amanuensis to raise money for Eldridge after town officials cheated her of some property. Both these texts present problems that make them useful in discussing African-American texts: the Grimes narrative illustrates the difficulties in the writing process for a self-taught former slave and the Eldridge book, written by a white woman, Frances Harriet Whipple, speaks to the problems of a different form of mediation: the transcriber, or amanuensis.

Students inured to graphic and violent representations are shocked when they move equipped with new insights concerning audience and rhetorical strategies to Grimes's narrative. Densely written without much coherent organization (for example, there are few paragraph breaks and no chapter breaks), the narrative first attracts students' notice through its aesthetic spareness and how its "homespun" nature reveals how much "craft" is required to write a seemingly seamless, or transparent, autobiography. More importantly, however, students notice how uncensored this narrator appears in contrast to Douglass. From its opening description of the narrator's white father—of whom Grimes is very proud, despite the father's evident insanity—to its ending in New Haven, Connecticut, on the grounds of Yale College, this narrative describes slave communities and slave masters warts and all. Grimes shares his relief on hearing the news that his first mistress had died— "thank God!"—discusses the cruelty of Black overseers, hints at the possibility of his sexual abuse by a master and another slave (in response to which he tries to break his own leg), and confesses to biting off the nose of another slave with an equanimity that bewilders modern readers. All these topics were taboo for abolitionists, who wanted to represent slaves to critical white readers as tractable, respectful, and hardworking; Grimes, in contrast, interpreted them all in his own picaresque and idiosyncratic way.

While Grimes obviously expects some sympathy of his readers, his opening gambit, in which he describes the purpose of the book as a purely financial one rather than an abolitionist one, makes it clear that Grimes positioned his narrative above all to sell, and to sell by entertaining. Whether they are sympathetic to Grimes or not (and this makes for very interesting class discussions!), students recognize how Grimes's narrative shows that Black writers addressed publics more concerned with enjoyment than with preaching about abolition and that this choice was an important and strategic one. They are also intrigued by the irony that even if potentially more scandalous, Grimes's narrative assumes its readers' identification with, rather than alienation from, its narrator. If Douglass appears in retrospect to have carefully and deliberately decided on each word he put down to prevent his audience from labeling him a member of an inferior race, Grimes's candid and sometimes disgustingly frank description of his experience as a slave shows that this former slave had cultivated an audience for whom his humanity, notwithstanding his rascality, was never in question. Students respond well to this dimension of the narrative since it is in many ways a more "realist" one than Douglass's, at the same time that they recognize how writers prior to 1845 might have had more flexibility in how they represented themselves and their purposes than later Black writers when abolition and slavery had become "mainstreamed" into the culture at large.

145

Grimes's narrative also offers insight into the roles that gender, class, and regional differences play in how Black writers address different audiences, in a manner analogous to the last autobiographical text that I teach in this course, Elleanor Eldridge's *Memoirs of Elleanor Eldridge.* This text exemplifies how gender and race and class converged to shape Black writers' rhetorical possibilities. This insight is all the more acute since this text was written by a white woman about a Black woman victimized, not as an impoverished former slave, but as a hardworking and successful entrepreneurial woman. If readers anticipate such a white-authored biography or "memoirs" to depict a textual version of abolition's kneeling slave, Whipple (the amanuensis) offers a strong and celebratory depiction of a Black working woman that contradicts conventional understandings of Black women as either victims or "drudges" and complements, rather than disparages, Eldridge's difference from the emerging dominant white middle-class ideal of "true womanhood."

The *Memoirs* offer important insights into the problems that successful African-Americans encountered in making a public appeal for economic justice in the "free" North. As the memoir of the first freeborn African-American we read, this text challenges students who want to insist on the freedom that slave narrators and narratives aspired to as a central, or even a sufficient, premise for a Black text. While some students, harrowed by Douglass's and Grimes's accounts of slavery's cruelty, come to invest themselves in the preeminence of abolition at the time, for the most part they recognize (as Grimes's narrative illustrated) that "freedom" was a contested term for African-Americans in many more complex ways than they had understood. From this perspective, Harriet Wilson's *Our Nig* would have also served this purpose (if not as autobiography then as "fiction"), but Eldridge's text is interesting in a way that the impoverished Wilson's is not: if antebellum race leaders and whites felt that the way to overcome racism was to cultivate exemplars of African-American industriousness and success, the defrauding of a hardworking and well-respected Black woman, as the narrator exclaims "simply because she is a colored woman," belies this claim.

Perhaps more importantly, however, the *Memoirs* testifies to the effective, even if often tense, nature of Eldridge and Whipple's interracial collaboration. While the text displays many tensions relating to the amanuensis and Eldridge's differing ideas of how discreet and/or how public the subject could be, Whipple's text portrays an otherwise unknown person and her story to great advantage. Whipple takes liberties in fictionalizing the scene of Eldridge's grandfather's captivity from Africa and in depicting the romance between Eldridge and her cousin (who died at sea) in sentimental terms that strike modern readers as "inauthentic." However, when they recognize these women's purpose —to raise money—and their audience—white middle-class women —students begin to appreciate this "poetic license." The unmarried Eldridge's resistance to her amanuensis's efforts to represent her within the generic conventions of the domestic heroine (she initially refuses to let Whipple read her romantic correspondence with her cousin) offers students insights into the difficulties of forging a language to represent a Black woman who exists outside conventions for race or femininity. How do you represent a defrauded, but prosperous, unmarried Black working woman to an audience for whom such women are, at best, invisible; at worst, degraded?

Travel narratives, a different form of autobiography, are the next genre on the syllabus that helps students appreciate how African-Americans, some slaves themselves, enjoyed limited forms of relatively uncoerced mobility. These texts illustrate Blacks' participation in an emerging middle-class adventure genre of travel literature while also showing how geographic mobility could influence an author's perception of his or her relation to nation, racial subjectivity, and representation. While this genre offers more choices—I can think of William Wells Brown's *Three Years in Europe*, for example, and David Dorr's *A Colored Man around the World*—I opt for texts by two freeborn northern women, Nancy Prince and Eliza Potter, that have very different geographic and discursive trajectories. Prince's 1850 *A Narrative of the life and travels of Mrs. Nancy Prince* (reprinted under the title *A Black Woman's Odyssey in Russia and Jamaica*) relates the story of Prince's impoverished childhood and adolescence in Massachusetts and her decision to marry an older man who worked in the court of the Russian czar as a member of a color guard. Eliza Potter's narrative describes a peripathetic and opinionated woman's travels as hairdresser to elite white women in Cincinnati, France, England, and posh resorts like Saratoga and New Orleans in the United States. Both narratives give students a sense of the wide range of Black women's texts for the period and challenge them to see Black working women in the light of their resilience and creativity in meeting the obstacles posed by their race, gender, class, and authorship. Though these women's decision to publish their stories potentially exposed them to derision by their white readers, they employed a variety of languages and forms to parry white readers' critical gaze and to represent their competence, knowledge, and "worldiness" to their readers.

Nancy Prince's *Life and Travels* piques students' interest because it opens with a racially conventional topic—the impoverished childhood and adolescence of a free Black woman—and then transitions at a marriage about which she says very little to an ethnographic and world traveler description of czarist Russia. This shift startles and intrigues modern readers because Prince's reticence to discuss what may have simply been a marriage of convenience that allowed her to escape her poverty (and the United States) leaves them wondering about what she does not say. Prince's representation of her stay in the czarist court (where her husband worked as a member of a security detail) traverses racial and class barriers since it depicts her as acquainted with the czarina, a client for Prince's business of children's clothes, and marks her as freely mobile and as an observer of Russian religious customs, a flood, and the Decembrist Revolt against the czar in 1826. Prince's transformation from impoverished woman to entrepreneurial world traveler in turn allows another shift in the text's trajectory. After returning to the United States on account of her health (a nice irony there, given that she feels "freer" in Russia) and her husband's subsequent death, Prince assumes the life of a race reformer principally involved in working with newly emancipated Jamaicans. Here the ambiguity and at times conflicting rhetorical goals of her publication (published primarily to support the impecunious Prince) become evident. As with Prince's earlier description of her departure from a United States in which she feels alienated, her account of her trips to Jamaica reads in part as a search for a "home" or sense of belonging that corresponds to her race and her values. While this account clearly refers to Prince's negotiations with U.S. racial hostility when she lives in the United States, ultimately Jamaica withholds fulfilling Prince's utopian hope for racial community as well. If nation—as in the United States—does not offer her a sense of belonging, Prince's Jamaican experience also suggests the problematic nature of assuming transnational racial affiliations from peoples of African descent who may share experiences of racial oppression but who are embedded in diverse Atlantic histories. The cautionary tale Prince's narrative offers about conditions in Jamaica also exemplifies this book's participation in debates about Black American emigration from this period that featured more well-known (and male) African-Americans.[3] From this perspective this text sheds light on the challenges that regional or class-based *intraracial* difference posed (and still poses) to our assumptions of diasporic transnational racial solidarity, or "imagined communities."

The significant role of travel narratives as sites for mediating and contextualizing African-Americans' racial and political commitments to the U.S. and other black communities also appears in a somewhat singular way in *A Hairdresser's Experience in High Life*, a narrative published in

1859 by Eliza Potter, a freeborn hairdresser who migrated to Cincinnati from New York. As such a migrant, Potter, through travel within the United States, is marked, as are thousands of others, as a participant in the young nation's western "expansion." As a traveler to Canada and to Europe, however, Potter is able to underscore and criticize the singularity and harshness of the U.S. racial order. While she does not go as far as William Wells Brown (who told British readers that English dogs saw him as more of a man than did Americans), Potter makes it clear that her travel abroad, like Prince's, was a key factor in authorizing her occupationally—she learned to dress hair in Paris—as well as socially. *A Hairdresser* offers students a fascinating look into the life and travels of a Black working woman who managed to accumulate sufficient cultural authority in her work with elite women to enable her to produce a frank and opinionated critique of clients who would have been considered her social superiors. This text surprises students who are curious about the source of her authority, never expecting that any Black woman could have said, much less published, such highly critical prose. *A Hairdresser* acknowledges the existence of slavery and racism in the United States (though Potter makes it clear she is not an "abolitionist" even if she is virulently antislavery) but otherwise makes little reference to the racially polarized public spheres in which we imagine all black-authored texts to have existed. Was she passing?, students want to know.

149

As with the Grimes narrative, *A Hairdresser* speaks to the existence of African-Americans' public authority outside abolition. In fact, it suggests how Black writers could succeed in representing themselves as participants in national discourses of citizenship, notwithstanding their political and cultural marginality. As readers in her day may have done, students appreciate Potter's arch put-down of social-climbing white women, marveling all the while at how she might have gotten away with such a feat (the reception of her text suggests that many agreed with her assessment of the period's "crisis" in confidence, in contrast to the reception of Elizabeth Keckley's *Behind the Scenes* nine years later). By leveraging the cosmopolitan experience, cultural authority, and skills that she had obtained in Europe and to which many Cincinnatians aspired, Potter exploited her readers' curiosity about how elite white women managed to convince her that they were "ladies" or not.

Respectability—who has it and who does not—represents a compelling framework for situating the two novels that I offer in this course. While Brown's 1853 novel *Clotel* operates very self-consciously on the ground of abolition, its innovative yoking of historical and fictional discourses, along with its highly episodic structure (as well as the prefacing third-person "Memoir" of Brown written by him), offers students a sense of the imaginative range that fiction permitted Black authors. The fact on which Brown insists—that white slave-owning men are respectable (even admired) at the same time that their progeny are making the rounds of slave markets—offers students a sense of how race *and* class have functioned to prevent deserving Blacks (some of them slaves of various complexions) from gaining their entitlements as American citizens. Though it is clear that the audience for this abolitionist novel was British, students understand how the novel's plot and characters make the case for transnational (not just raced or abolitionist) norms of heroism and respectability.

Frank Webb's *The Garies and their Friends* shows students the northern U.S. version of a text that imagines a "middle class" (always posed in a somewhat problematic light) Black community that is well deserving yet constantly under threat of violence. It is a little off-putting (even though not surprising) to contend with students' open stupefaction that hardworking Blacks could be what we might call "middle class" and that African-Americans could speak and enact forms of propriety that they do not even necessarily associate with middle class, but rather with whiteness. The imminent and realistic violence Webb depicts as threatening (and in some cases killing and maiming) northern Blacks offers students a context for understanding how class and race (as white) have been conflated in formations of U.S. citizenship, while again (as with *Clotel* and other texts) illustrating the relevance of reading and writing publics outside those of abolition. (Because the text focused exclusively on the plight of respectable northern Blacks, it was largely ignored by abolitionists.) It also dramatizes how modern interpretive frameworks about the Black "bourgeoisie," inherited from the sociologist E. Franklin Frazier and the like, have little, if any, relation to antebellum historical contexts and the representational strategies available to Black authors.

The implications of Black authors' access to different representational strategies are traced out in provocative fashion in the last genre we read in this course: texts that I call *condition* or *protosociological.* In this section we read Joseph Willson's *Sketches of the Higher Classes of Colored Society* (Philadelphia, 1841) and Cyprian Clamorgan's *The Colored Aristocracy of St. Louis* (St. Louis, 1858)—texts that chronicle the habits and ideas of a class of people with whom the nation as a whole was then entirely unfamiliar: the "higher classes" and the "colored aristocracy." Clamorgan and Willson (whom I've designated *chroniclers* to point out the similarities and the differences between these authors and professional sociologists) linked African-Americans to classed identities in efforts to revise homogenizing notions of racial degradation that assumed, as Willson complained, that "The sight of one colored man . . . is the sight of a community." These two texts offer two very different yet complementary schemas of intraracial difference that focus our emphasis on *representations* of raced class, in this way preempting students' tendency to read unfamiliar African-American texts sociologically—that is, as merely attesting to the existence of class difference among Blacks. These texts show how understandings of intraracial class could be seen as relevant to efforts to legitimize African-Americans individually and as members of a group. If Black and white abolitionists were seeking to tap the collectivizing potential of racial identity and subjectivity, these Black authors point to the cultural work that difference within the race could perform. They also highlight how such difference could function (counterintuitively) as a rhetorical ground for Blacks' political and cultural mobilization.

151

Though written in highly formal nineteenth-century polite prose, Willson's text has a modern flavor that stems in part from its quasi-empirical claims and methods. Willson assumes his readers' ignorance of the African-American social dynamics he describes—the literary and temperance societies, the polite visiting, and the educational attainments and propriety that this population displays. To counter the burlesque parodying of middle-class blacks prevalent in minstrelsy and visual media, Willson seeks to establish the existence of such a class (not without its imperfections, of course) in ways that today's students also view with interest. His book counters received opinions about the pri-

macy of race over class and gender in Black communities in ways that
students perceive as still relevant and full of implications and yields new
light on the constitutive role of intersecting race and class and gender
formations in U.S. social structure. The book's methods and contexts
prompt interesting questions pertaining to race in popular and cultural
representational fields today. What happens if we openly acknowledge
the existence of intraracial class difference rather than seeing it as a
symptom of false consciousness or racial self-loathing? Does the notion
of racial particularity or blackness itself disappear? Does such a recognition deprive us of an important rhetorical ground for negotiating and
reshaping oppressive U.S. racial orders?

Cyprian Clamorgan's provocative 1858 book *The Colored Aristocracy
of St. Louis*, like the Willson text, also intervenes in national depictions
of African-Americans' cultural significance and political powerlessness.
In *Colored Aristocracy*, published after the 1857 U.S. Supreme Court
decision of *Scott v. Sandford* (Dred Scott was originally from St. Louis),
Clamorgan claims that national representations of African-American
communities are highly "romantic." He singles out *Uncle Tom's Cabin* and
the narratives of fugitive slaves as examples of this literary romanticism,
insisting instead on his paradoxical belief that "elite" African-Americans,
though deprived of the franchise, exercise political influence in U.S.
politics on account of their money. For his purposes, the existence of the
"colored aristocracy" that he describes—giving names and addresses and
pithy descriptions—is proof that notwithstanding national efforts to
dominate African-Americans (free Blacks, as well as slaves) some members of this population have managed to extract some measure of wealth,
and by implication, some measure of legitimacy in the teeth of their
oppression. Alternatively humorous, ironic, and earnest, this inventory
of the Black elite in a southern city illustrates the regional specificity of
a culturally diverse Black community (Clamorgan himself was of French
descent) that embraces a highly stratified society as proof, not of its
blackness, but of its legitimacy and its "Americanness." In this text,
regional political and national "representativeness" displaces any imperative to racial "representativeness."

As do all the texts of this course, Clamorgan's *Colored Aristocracy*
dramatizes the provocative possibilities antebellum African-American

texts offer when they are not organized around the traditional slavery- and abolition-centered schema. This list of texts could also include poetry—the poets James Whitfield and George Moses Horton come to mind—as well as any other number of unconventional texts that challenge our assumptions about African-American authorship in the United States. The point is to complicate students' understandings of what constitute raced texts and Black authors' audiences so that they can better appreciate the multiple or heterogeneous traditions African-American writers inaugurated and revised.

Notes

1. Langston Hughes, "The Negro Artist and the Racial Mountain," published in *The Nation* (1926), 692–94.

2. "Frederick Douglass and the American Jeremiad," excerpted from Andrews's influential book, *To Tell A Free Story* (Champaign: University of Illinois Press, 1986) and reprinted in the Norton Critical Edition of *Narrative of the Life of Frederick Douglass, an American Slave*, ed. by William L. Andrews and William S. McFeely (New York: Norton, 1997).

3. Sandra Gunning, "Nancy Prince and the Politics of Mobility, Home and Diasporic (Mis) Identification," *American Quarterly* 53, no. 1 (March 2001): 32–69.

Robert S. Levine

*M*onuments and Careers: Teaching William Wells Brown, Martin Delany, and Their Contemporaries

MOST UNDERGRADUATE LITERATURE COURSES ARE SURVEYS of one sort or another in which coverage remains the course's donné, aspiration, and, if all goes well, achievement. Given that the majority of our students have not read widely, it certainly makes sense to encourage them to read as much as possible. But comprehensiveness exacts a price, and not just because the headlong exposure to numerous texts allows insufficient time for close reading. Surveys work with canons, and, whether traditional or revisionary, canons in survey courses tend to consist of single works by a number of writers, therefore cutting off fuller consideration of the place of individual works in relation to writers' larger careers. The result is that the individual works become monuments of sorts while individual careers become invisible or irrelevant. Students thus lose sight of the flux and conflict that mark most writing careers and have little understanding of possible changes in authors' ideological perspectives and representational strategies. Students who read only Harriet Beecher Stowe's *Uncle Tom's Cabin* (1852), for instance, learn about that novel's politics of racialism and colonizationism but in all likelihood will hear nothing about Stowe's subsequent antislavery novel *Dred* (1856), in which she renounced colonizationism and confuted aspects of the racialism so central to *Uncle Tom's Cabin*. In the context of the survey course, Stowe's views as they informed her most influential novel are Stowe's views—period.

Were Stowe able to leap forward to our present moment, she would probably understand all of the attention devoted to *Uncle Tom's Cabin* because that novel did define her subsequent career. But if we could offer some of our canonical African-American writers similar opportunities to look over our shoulders, would they be able to understand the attention paid to just one or two of their works? Consider Frederick Douglass. His *Narrative of the Life of Frederick Douglass* appeared in 1845 when he was twenty-seven years old. Since the 1960s, as Deborah E. McDowell has pointed out, that text has had a "monumental status" in African-American literary and cultural studies, thereby contributing to Douglass's own monumental status in the field as *the* representative African-American.[1] Although the *Narrative* had an absolutely crucial place in Douglass's emergence as an antislavery leader in the camp of William Lloyd Garrison, the fact is that it went out of print in 1849 and was not back in print until 1960.[2] How important was that text between 1850 and 1960, or, to focus just on Douglass's career, how important was that text to Douglass after 1851, the year he officially broke with Garrison? Douglass lived for fifty years after the publication of *Narrative*, wrote hundreds of essays and speeches and even a novella, edited newspapers, and published revised and expanded versions of his autobiography. The odds are that he would be baffled by the almost single-minded attention that we give to a book that preceded what he regarded as the most significant decades of his career.

This chapter argues for a teaching practice that attends to the complex shifts and turns of African-American literary and political careers. To focus on single texts either distorts or occludes the place of the text in the often pragmatically driven careers of African-American writers who, especially before 1865, regarded their writing as part of their ongoing efforts to challenge white supremacist slave culture. To be sure, time and scheduling realities will continue to make single texts the focus of survey and other comprehensive courses on African-American writing. But even single works can be studied in relation to careers. My focus will be on William Wells Brown and Martin R. Delany, an emphasis that may appear to be self-serving, insofar as I will be suggesting ways of studying Brown's and Delany's respective careers with the help of editions I have prepared on these writers. But these editions emerged from my thinking about the issues addressed in this essay, and I believe that, whenever possible, the best way of addressing African-Americans' literary careers is through an examination of original print contexts: African-American newspapers, convention transcripts, and the like.

I begin with William Wells Brown's *Clotel; or, The President's Daughter* (1853), which is, as far as we know, the first novel published by an African-American. As a "first," it has achieved monumental status in the canon of African-American writing and is regularly taught in surveys of African-American literature and in courses on the history of the African-American and the American novel. According to my check of the *Books in Print* database on June 1, 2006, there are currently eight different editions of *Clotel* in print, including new editions from Penguin and Dover, compared to nine editions of what are by my count Brown's fifteen other works, not including his numerous speeches, essays, and various editions and republications of his books (over a two-year period he published at least four editions of his history *The Black Man*, for instance).[3] Prior to *Clotel*, Brown published *Narrative of William W. Brown* (1847); *A Lecture Delivered before the Female Anti-Slavery Society of Salem* (1847); an edition of antislavery songs, *The Anti-Slavery Harp* (1848); *A Description of William Well's Brown's Original Panoramic Views of the Scenes in the Life of An American Slave* (1850), which in fascinating ways links word and image; and an engaging and (given its Black subject) unusual travel narrative, *Three Years in Europe* (1852). After *Clotel*, Brown published three considerably revised and reconceived versions of the novel, *Miralda; or, The Beautiful Quadroon* (1860–61), *Clotelle: A Tale of the Southern States* (1864), and *Clotelle; or, The Colored Heroine* (1867); a more expansive narrative of his travels in Europe, *The American Fugitive in Europe* (1855); a play, *The Escape* (1858); numerous speeches, including *St. Domingo: Its Revolution and Its Patriots* (1855); memoirs and autobiographical narratives such as *Memoir of William Wells Brown* (1859) and *My Southern Home* (1880); and several histories, including *The Black Man* (1863) and *The Rising Son* (1874). In addition to these books and tracts, Brown published hundreds of contributions in the periodical press of the time, such as letters, reportage, and transcripts of his speeches. Amid all of this activity, there is absolutely no indication in any of Brown's writings that he regarded the 1853 *Clotel* as having a special status in his career. If anything, his revisions and reconceptualizations of the novel during the 1860s suggest that he began to see the novel as rather limited, and his move to history in the 1860s and 1870s suggests that he saw historical recovery as a more vital form of writing than fiction.

This is not to say that *Clotel* does not deserve our close attention. But the evidence suggests that Brown saw it as but one of many texts in an ongoing literary and political career, a novel that, as is true for all of his writings, continues to speak to us beyond the confines of its historical moment but was nonetheless a rhetorical performance that had a particular purpose at a particular time and place, 1853 London, where the novel was published. (It was not republished in the United States until the 1960s.) Having sailed to Liverpool in 1849 in order to attend the International Peace Conference in Paris, Brown chose to remain in England after the passage of the Fugitive Slave Law in 1850. In 1853 he met Harriet Beecher Stowe in London, and *Clotel* may have been prompted by a desire to respond to *Uncle Tom's Cabin.* But the novel was also clearly motivated by his sense that he could take advantage of his increasing fame in England as a lecturer and writer in order to persuade white British readers to continue to work for the antislavery cause in the United States. As he writes in the preface to the novel: "If the incidents set forth in the following pages . . . should thereby aid in bringing British influence to bear upon American slavery, the main object for which this work was written will have been accomplished."[4] Rather than aspiring in Melvillean fashion to write "the Gospels in this century,"[5] Brown in *Clotel* sought to do cultural work by attempting to instruct and influence his white British readers. The rhetorical aims of the novel help to explain its odd racial politics, such as its occasional use of minstrel humor, its seeming valuing of light-complected Blacks over dark-complected Blacks, and especially its escapist conclusion, which presents the two light-complected former slaves who have emerged as the novel's heroine and hero living happily ever after as nonraced Blacks in Europe. Had Brown imagined African-American readers or U.S. abolitionists as his primary readers, he may well have fashioned a different ending that would have had more to say about the situation of the slaves in the United States.

When Brown returned to the United States in 1854, his attention turned to the situation of Blacks in the Americas, and we can discern a marked change from the color politics of the 1853 *Clotel*. Brown's great 1855 speech, *St. Domingo*, displayed his interest in Black revolutionism in the Americas (which he anticipated in the brief portrayal of the "full-blooded negro"[6] Picquilo in *Clotel*) and points to his emerging interest in Black emigration to Haiti. Just before the outbreak of the Civil War, Brown began actively working for African-American emigration to Haiti, and he continued to work for Haitian emigration during the war's first year, serving as a contributing editor to the *Pine and Palm*, a newspaper devoted to Haitian emigration, and lecturing widely on the subject in the United States and Canada. During this same time he dramatically reconceived *Clotel* for serial publication in the *Weekly Anglo-African*, an African-American newspaper published in New York City. The new narrative, titled *Miralda; or, The Beautiful Quadroon: A Romance of American Slavery*, appeared in the issues of December 1, 1860, to March 16, 1861. Brown made a number of changes from *Clotel* to *Miralda* reflective of the considerably different political and print contexts of 1853 and 1860–61: he jettisoned his collage narrative technique for a more traditional narrative storytelling, extended the tale past the European reunion and marriage that conclude *Clotel*, and made the book's Black male hero Black to the eye. In short, Brown authored a Black nationalist novel that had little apparent interest in addressing white readers.

And yet by 1862, Brown embraced the Civil War as a war of emancipation. Abandoning his Haitian emigrationism, he published a revision of *Miralda, Clotelle: A Tale of the Southern States*, in a series of books intended for Union soldiers and their sympathizers. In this 1864 version of the novel, Brown provides an "interracial" conclusion in which the light-complected Black woman and dark-complected Black man choose to return to the United States after reconciling with the woman's white father. The expectation is that the Black man, Jerome, will fight in the Civil War, and Brown's clear rhetorical aim is to show that African

159

Americans should be part of the Union military effort. Given Blacks' heroic participation in the war, however, Brown became disillusioned with Reconstruction in the South, and in his final revision of the novel, *Clotelle; or, The Colored Heroine,* published in 1867, he expressed his despair at the anti-Black racism that remained endemic to the culture, portraying the pointless deaths of Jerome and more than ten other African-American soldiers who are killed while attempting to fulfill a white officer's command to retrieve the dead body of a white officer. The nation's failure to confront that racism would become one of the central concerns of his subsequent histories and memoirs.

Clotel, then, tells only a small part of Brown's story, and it is most usefully read, I think, in relation to his ongoing, conflicted, and some-times contradictory thinking about race, slavery, and nation. That said, given the novel's status as a "first," it makes sense that students enrolled in a course on the history of the African-American novel would begin with *Clotel.* Those same students would then move fairly quickly to

160

Martin R. Delany's *Blake; or The Huts of America: A Tale of the Mississippi Valley, the Southern United States, and Cuba* (1859, 1861–62), which they would read in the Beacon Press edition published in 1970—currently the only extant edition of the novel.[7] This edition, which is riddled with textual errors, fails to give the novel's subtitle but more impor-tantly, and understandably, fails to convey the material reality of the novel that its contemporaneous readers would have encountered. Holding it in their hands, students would regard this work as just another approximately three-hundred-page novel that they would have to read and analyze during a typically difficult semester. But what exactly is *Blake* and where does it fit in Delany's career? For one thing, it is a two-part novel that was not published in book form. Most of part 1 was published in the 1859 New York–based *Anglo-African Magazine;* then during 1861–62 most of the overall novel, like *Miralda,* was pub-lished in the New York *Weekly Anglo-African,* though we are missing the issues that presumably have the novel's closing chapters.

While *Blake* tends to be the one work that undergraduates in English departments read by Delany, the facts suggest, as with Brown's *Clotel,* that Delany did not regard this novel as a particularly important part of his career. At the very least, this is not the work that he wanted to be known for. Like Brown, Delany published hundreds of essays and letters in the Black press; he also published eight books and pamphlets in addition to the serialized *Blake*, including *The Condition, Elevation, Emigration, and Destiny of the Colored People of the United States* (1852), *Official Report of the Niger Valley Exploring Party* (1861), and *Principia of Ethnology* (1879). In her 1868 biography, which she wrote in collaboration with Delany, Frances Rollin discusses and prints selections from a number of Delany's writings, including the complete text of his call for Black emigration, "Political Destiny of the Colored Race on the American Continent" (1854).[8] But she does not have a word to say about *Blake*, presumably because Delany chose not to talk to her about the novel. If Delany did not regard *Blake* as a significant part of his career, then why do we monumentalize his only novel at the expense of the many other writings that he valued equally or more?

To address this question, it would be helpful to be as precise as possible about the place of *Blake* in Delany's career. During the late 1840s, Delany worked with Frederick Douglass as coeditor of the abolitionist newspaper the *North Star* and shared his Garrisonian commitment to moral suasion and Black uplift in the United States. But in the late 1840s Delany left the newspaper and increasingly positioned himself against what he regarded as Douglass's naive accommodationism. Disillusioned by the Compromise of 1850, Delany in *Condition* argued that Blacks should consider emigrating to Central and South America; that same year he debated Frederick Douglass in the pages of *Frederick Douglass' Paper* on the merits of *Uncle Tom's Cabin*, arguing, contra Douglass, who championed Stowe, that the novel was racist. Eric J. Sundquist and Jean Fagan Yellin have speculated that Delany began *Blake* in 1852 or 1853 as a response to *Uncle Tom's Cabin*, with the aim of portraying plantation Blacks as more inclined toward revolutionary violence than Stowe would have wanted to suggest.[9] But though some of the early chapters may have been drafted shortly after Delany read sections of *Uncle Tom's Cabin*, the descriptions of Blacks in Canada later in part I suggest that Delany may have done his main work on the novel sometime between 1856 and 1859 when he was living in Canada. Read in that context, the novel has an expanded view of Blacks' place in the Americas, suggestive of Delany's initial enthusiasm for life in Canada and his continued support for Black emigration. As a post-1856 novel, *Blake* could also be read as an admiring response to Stowe's second anti-slavery novel, *Dred*, which, like *Blake*, has as a dark-complected Black revolutionary hero and an affirmative picture of a thriving Black settlement in Canada. The possibility of a post-1856 composition also suggests that the novel may have been informed by Delany's anger and despair at the 1857 Dred Scott decision, and his subsequent attraction to the revolutionary politics of John Brown. If Delany did his primary work on the novel in 1858, for example, that would be around the same time he chaired a Black convention in Chatham, Canada West, that enthusiastically supported Brown's mission to organize the slaves' resistance. Delany presented the manuscript of the novel to Thomas Hamilton, editor of the *Anglo-African Magazine*, six months after that convention, and Hamilton, before beginning the serialization, initially printed three chapters in the January 1859 issue, telling his readers that Delany's novel portrayed a violent uprising against the white slave power as inspired by "a deep laid organization" of conspiratorial Blacks.[10] Had Delany printed all of *Blake* that year and actually joined Brown, we would no doubt be reading the novel in relation to the attack on Harpers Ferry.

162

But one month after selections from *Blake* appeared in the *Anglo-African Magazine*, Delany wrote to William Lloyd Garrison asking him to read those chapters, hoping that Garrison's enthusiasm would help him "to get a good publishing house to take it" so that he could "make a penny by it."[11] Delany dreamed of making the sort of money that he imagined Stowe made from *Uncle Tom's Cabin* because he now wanted additional funding for his Niger Exploring Expedition, which sought to establish an African-American colony in West Africa. Rather than joining Brown's rebellion at Harpers Ferry, Delany departed for Africa in July 1859 and by the end of the year had signed a treaty with tribal leaders for land in the Yoruba region. He then toured England in search of funds for the project, and he returned to Canada in 1861 to recruit Black emigrants for his African community. Failing to find a New York firm willing to publish *Blake*, Delany offered the complete manuscript to Hamilton, who began the serialization in the *Weekly Anglo-African* in the issue of November 23, 1861. This may or may not have been the same manuscript that Delany gave to Hamilton in 1858 or 1859. Although there are only small differences between the twenty-five chapters that Hamilton published in 1859 and republished in 1861, there are a number of "authenticating" footnotes in the Africa section of the novel's second part suggesting that Delany had reconceived aspects of *Blake* during 1861 in order to bring it more into accord with his hopes of developing a regenerative African-American community in Africa. But with the outbreak of the Civil War, and increasing signs that the projected community was collapsing for lack of funding, the serialization may well have seemed increasingly irrelevant to Black readers, and perhaps to Delany himself. Scholars speculate that there are six chapters of the novel in the missing May 1862 issues of the paper. Did Delany revise any of those chapters in light of his emerging interest in supporting the Union side of the Civil War? By 1863 Delany was actively engaged in recruiting Black troops, and in 1864 Lincoln named him the first Black major in the Union army. Embracing northern Unionism, Delany perhaps wished to conceal his authorship of a Black revolutionary novel when, as an official at the Freedmen's Bureau in South Carolina, he reviewed his life history with Francis Rollin in 1867. Had she interviewed him in the late 1870s, after he became convinced of the failure of Reconstruction and was once again attempting to promote Black emigration to Africa, he may well have had something to say about *Blake.*

Given *Blake*'s and *Clotel*'s multiple and conflicting sources, purposes, contexts, and audiences, we need to be wary of developing univocal or overly constricted formalist readings of these novels. My point is not that we should devalue *Blake* or *Clotel*, for both are wonderfully complex and challenging novels. But in order to take their full measure, we need to see them as part of the writers' ongoing political and literary work in the Americas. Neither Brown nor Delany was aspiring to produce masterpieces for the ages; they were using their writing to think through issues and accomplish political ends. Their novels were part of unfolding careers that continued to unfold until Brown and Delany wrote their final words. A career criticism that considers political, historical, and, most importantly, rhetorical contexts best helps to illuminate the achievements and limitations of these activists and writers.

As an editor of Brown and of Delany, I have sought to present texts in relation to careers, and I want briefly now to suggest how my paying attention to print contexts can help to encourage considerations of *Clotel* and *Blake* in relation to the larger arc of authorial careers. Though my essay begins with an implied complaint about the surfeit of editions of *Clotel*, I confess to having contributed to the problem by editing a Bedford Cultural Edition of *Clotel*, which was published in 2000. The aim of Bedford Cultural Editions is to historicize texts for student readers, and one of my goals in the *Clotel* edition was to accomplish that end by providing readers with a number of the sources that Brown drew on for his pastiche of a novel. Accordingly, the edition includes, among many other items, Lydia Maria Child's "The Quadroons" (1842), which Brown liberally "plagiarized"; Grace Greenwood's poem "The Leap from the Long Bridge" (1851), which inspired a key scene in the novel; several texts about Jefferson's fathering of slave children; and some of the proslavery writings that Brown quotes word for word, such as Thomas Bacon's *Sermons Addressed to Masters and Servants* (1813), in order to point to their cruelty and blindness. The availability of these sources allows readers to see how Brown appropriated, transformed, and ironically recontextualized texts that were circulating in his culture.

164

But I also wanted to give readers a sense of *Clotel*'s place in Brown's still developing career—as a rhetorical effort, response, and performance of 1853 that was but one of his many and varied responses to the crisis of slavery and racism in the United States. The edition has a selection from Brown's relatively familiar Garrisonian *Narrative* and from his more obscure and cosmopolitan *A Description of William Wells Brown's Original Panoramic Views*, works that are important antecedents to *Clotel*. But my emphasis was on documenting Brown's shifting racial and political views after the publication of *Clotel*, and the ways those views contributed to his subsequent reconceptualizations of the novel. Thus I provide a selection from his 1855 speech *St. Domingo*, backgrounds on his increasing interest in Haiti, excerpts from texts that show his renewed commitment to the Civil War as a war of emancipation (such as the transcript of a Black convention he attended in 1864 and his 1867 *The Negro in the American Rebellion*), and chapters from his two versions of *Clotelle* that help readers to see how he reconceived his first novel. Brown's frustrations with the U.S. nation, along with his hopes, are put in focus in his 1880 *My Southern Home*, a text that shows Brown continuing to engage issues of race and nation. Students reading *Clotel* in this edition would therefore see the novel as a way station, or stopping ground, a novel that poses particular problems for particular audiences at a particular time. In this larger volume, there is no fixed or absolutely set vision of race or nation. There are conflict, dialogue, hope, and despair.[12]

Conflict is also crucial to my *Martin R. Delany: A Documentary Reader*, though the word I emphasize in the edition, in order to accent Delany's canny rhetorical efforts, is *improvisation*.[13] The volume highlights six discrete career moments, ranging from Delany's newspaper editing and freemasonry work in Pittsburgh, to his coediting of the *North Star* with Douglass, to his Central and South American emigrationism, to his African emigrationism, to his Civil War and Reconstruction efforts, and finally to his promotion of Liberian emigrationism in the late 1870s. These are somewhat arbitrary and overlapping divisions, of course, intended to provide readers with a relatively clear picture of Delany's moves through various abolitionisms, emigrationisms, and other antiracist and antislavery activities. But the fact is that Delany did make impassioned commitments at particular historical moments, and those commitments changed with historical circumstances. Readers interested in Delany's writing career apart from (or in addition to) *Blake* would find this volume especially useful, allowing as it does for the study of Delany as a writer of letters and essays, such as "True Patriotism" and "Southern Customs." The edition also provides a sampling of Delany's emigrationist and travel writings ("Political Destiny" and excerpts from *Condition* and *Official Report*), his Civil War and Reconstruction writings ("Monument to President Lincoln," *University Pamphlets*, "The South and Its Foes"), and his writings on race ("Africa and the African Race," *Principia of Ethnology*, and many others), along with excerpts from *Blake*.

165

The edition would also work well for those interested in teaching all of *Blake* in the context of Delany's career. For my own classes on *Blake*, I have put the documentary edition on reserve and have called my students' attention to the following materials: Delany's *The Origin and Objects of Ancient Freemasonry* (1853), which helps to illuminate his mystical conception of Blake's quest for a Black diasporic leadership; his writings on Cuba, such as "Annexation of Cuba" and "The Redemption of Cuba" (both from 1849), which anticipate his account of Cuba in *Blake*; and his epistolary debate of 1853 with Frederick Douglass on Stowe's *Uncle Tom's Cabin*, which helps students to see how Delany may have begun work on the novel in order to challenge Stowe's racialism. In addition to calling students' attention to important source materials, I want them to have a clearer picture of how the novel emerged from Delany's competing career interests. To that end, I have them read some of his emigrationist writings, such as *Condition* and "Political Destiny," so they can see the key place of hemispheric politics in his literary imagination, but I also urge them to look at his writings on Canada and, especially, Africa, such as his 1861 *Official Report*. Finally, I want them to see the overlap of *Blake*'s publication history, including the missing chapters of 1862, with Delany's turn to the Union side of the Civil War, and I have them read Rollin's account (based on Delany's) of his meeting with President Lincoln in 1864, which led to his appointment as major. Here they can see how Delany's interest in Black revolutionary leadership actually culminated (for a time) in a renewed U.S. nationalism that both draws on and works against the grain of the heroic Black leadership that Delany limns in *Blake*. Overall, these readings help to make clear that *Blake* expresses sometimes competing longings and commitments and is in many ways an amalgam of Delany's and other African-Americans' desires and political efforts during what could be termed the long mid-nineteenth century.

I have been suggesting, then, that there are a number of compelling reasons for moving from a pedagogy of monuments to a pedagogy of careers. I want to conclude by highlighting three aspects of African-American literary study and pedagogy that would be well served by such a shift in emphasis:

1) The Nation: During a time in which critics are pointing to the limits of the nation as a unit of literary analysis, we continue to look at African-American writers in relatively fixed and set terms in relation to the nation. Douglass, for example, is regularly portrayed as the nationalist par excellence, while Delany is regularly portrayed as the Black nationalist emigrationist with an "African dream."[14] Career study reveals the nation to be an ongoing question for a number of African-American

writers as they, in effect, write across the nation. Douglass, for instance, was tempted by Haitian emigration in the late 1850s and wrote one of his great transnational speeches, "The Significance of Emancipation in the West Indies" (1857), during this time. Because of the centrality of Jefferson's Declaration to Brown's *Clotel*, that novel, too, has commonly been read with respect to the ideals of the U.S. nation. But again, when Brown moves toward a Haitian emigrationism, all that changes, as he actually drops all mention of Jefferson from his 1860s revisions. Brown's reembrace of the United States during the Civil War thus was not more of the same but part of his new thinking about how to link a politics of emancipation to the Civil War. Delany at various points in his career similarly sought to link African-Americans' fortunes to the U.S. nation even as he continued to map out various emigration projects. Focusing exclusively on Douglass's *Narrative*, Brown's *Clotel*, or Delany's *Blake* obscures the tug and pull of nation during these writers' long and complicated careers.

2) Gender: Career study makes clear the significant differences between the situations of male and female African-American writers during the nineteenth century. Male writers such as David Walker, Douglass, Delany, Brown, Henry Highland Garnet, James Holly, and many others had public roles in relation to various Black and white antislavery organizations. Quests for leadership were often absolutely central to their work, as these male writers were often arguing with one another; thus it is not surprising that tropes of representativeness and leadership inform their writings. The color politics of *Clotel*, for example, has a lot to do with Brown's own experience of being a light-complected Black in U.S. and British reform communities; the conception of the heroic dark-complected Blake is intimately tied to the dark-complected Delany's fantasies of Black Masonic leadership. In their own ways, African-American women writers such as Maria Stewart, Sojourner Truth, and Frances Harper went public, but they were usually working apart from institutions or with those church institutions that called on women to keep out of the public eye (even as they resisted those calls). Career criticism encourages us to address these differences along the lines of gender and to explore the significance of such differences in the writings themselves.

3) Teaching the Conflicts: African-American literary and political careers were careers in conflict. Gerald Graff argues that we should "teach the conflicts"—by which he means the current interpretive conflicts specific to particular texts and to current debates in literary studies.[15] But Graff's model assumes that critics on either side have settled visions of writers and texts, whereas career criticism unsettles such basic assumptions. Instead, the conflicts that one might teach are not those between, say, liberal and conservative readers in the early twenty-first century but rather the internal conflicts marking particular careers as they unfolded over time in the nineteenth century. Brown, for example, remained in conflict about race throughout his career, while Delany remained in conflict about nation. Furthermore, because Brown and Delany were both public leaders, they were in conflict with a number of other African-American leaders of the time. Too often we present Black-authored texts as troping or signifying on white culture, but the fact is that there was extraordinary diversity of opinion in the African-American community, and Black writers were often responding to other Black writers. Much of Delany's work is a response to Douglass's (just as a good deal of what Douglass wrote responds to Delany). Similarly, Brown and Delany disputed with one another, and their arguments over Haitian versus African emigration during the late 1850s and early 1860s may well have had an impact on their writing of *Clotelle* and *Blake*, respectively.[16]

When one teaches African-American "monuments" in relation to African-American careers, nothing is static, ideas and representational strategies are always in flux, and the work under consideration ultimately exists in relation to a variety of traditions and contexts, including what I would term its revisionary future. In part, that future is our present moment. Thinking about texts dynamically as always in process allows for the perpetual possibility of new revisionary possibilities, a perspective that allows for a greater interpretive freedom to engage texts as part of an ongoing cultural conversation. This change in interpretive perspective has a special relevance to the teaching of nineteenth-century African-American literature because the texts themselves were so engaged with finding ways of challenging the status quo. Career criticism in the African-American literature classroom, I would like to think, can only encourage students to take a more active role in making their own rhetorically savvy interventions in the status quo, both as critical readers and as citizens working toward a more fully democratic culture.

Notes

1. Deborah E. McDowell, "In the First Place: Making Frederick Douglass and the Afro-American Narrative Tradition," in *Critical Essays on Frederick Douglass*, ed. William L. Andrews, 193 (Boston: G. K. Hall, 1991). On representativeness, see also Rafia Zafar, "Franklinian Douglass: The Afro-American as Representative Man," in *Frederick Douglass: New Literary and Historical Essays*, ed. Eric J. Sundquist, 114–65 (New York: Cambridge University Press, 1990); Wilson J. Moses, "Where Honor Is Due: Frederick Douglass as Representative Black Man," *Prospects* 17 (1992): 177–89; and Robert S. Levine, *Martin Delany, Frederick Douglass, and the Politics of Representative Identity* (Chapel Hill: University of North Carolina Press, 1997).

2. Frederick Douglass, *Narrative of the Life of Frederick Douglass, An American Slave, Written by Himself*, ed. Benjamin Quarles (Cambridge, MA: Harvard University Press, 1960).

3. I do not claim absolute accuracy of this count, as Brown's *Narrative* is included in several collections of antislavery narratives. But this count does give a good sense of relative emphasis.

4. William Wells Brown, *Clotel; or, The President's Daughter*, ed. Robert S. Levine, 47 (Boston: Bedford/St. Martin's, 2000). The best biography of Brown remains William Edward Farrison, *William Wells Brown: Author and Reformer* (Chicago: University of Chicago Press, 1969).

5. Herman Melville to Nathaniel Hawthorne, letter of June 1, 1851, in Melville, *Correspondence*, ed. Lynn Horth, 192 (Evanston and Chicago: Northwestern University Press and The Newberry Library, 1993).

6. Brown, *Clotel*, p. 201.

7. Martin R. Delany, *Blake; or, The Huts of America*, ed. Floyd J. Miller (Boston: Beacon Press, 1970).

8. Frank [Frances] Rollin, *Life and Public Services of Martin R. Delany* (Boston: Lee and Shepard, 1868).

9. See Jean Fagan Yellin, *The Intricate Knot: Black Figures in American Literature, 1776–1863* (New York: New York University Press, 1972), 193–211; and Eric J. Sundquist, *To Wake the Nations: Race in the Making of American Literature* (Cambridge, MA: Harvard University Press, 1993), chap. 2, esp. 192–94.

10. The *Anglo-African Magazine*, January 1859, p. 20. For a fuller discussion of the various contexts of *Blake*, see Levine, *Martin Delany, Frederick Douglass*, chap. 5.

11. Delany to William Lloyd Garrison, letter of February 19, 1859, in *Martin R. Delany: A Documentary Reader*, ed. Robert S. Levine 295 (Chapel Hill: University of North Carolina Press, 2003).

12. Also useful in this regard is the recently published reader *The Works of William Wells Brown: Using His "Strong, Manly Voice,"* ed. Paula Garrett and Hollis Robbins (New York: Oxford University Press, 2006).

13. On the improvisatory dimension of Delany's career, see Levine, "Introduction," in *Martin R. Delany*, 1–22.

169

14. See, for example, Cyril E. Griffith, *The African Dream: Martin R. Delany and the Emergence of Pan-African Thought* (University Park: Pennsylvania State University Press, 1975).

15. Gerald Graff, *Beyond the Culture Wars: How Teaching the Conflicts Can Revitalize American Education* (New York: W. W. Norton, 1992).

16. See Victor Ullman, *Martin R. Delany: The Beginnings of Black Naitonalism* (Boston: Beacon Press, 1971), 255; and *Martin R. Delany*, ed. Levine, esp. 368–69.

Contributors

VINCENT CARRETTA is Professor of English at the University of Maryland. He is the author of *Equiano, the African: Biography of a Self-Made Man* (2005), which won the Annibel Jenkins Prize for Best Biography of the Year. He is editor of Phillis Wheatley's *Complete Writings*, Equiano's *The Interesting Narrative*, and Ignatius Sancho's *Letters*, each for Penguin-Putnam. In addition to numerous articles, he edited the collection *Unchained Voices: An Anthology of Black Authors in the English-Speaking World of the Eighteenth Century* (1996; revised and expanded 2004).

MICHAEL J. DREXLER is Assistant Professor of English at Bucknell University. His edition of Leonora Sansay's *Secret History; or the Horrors of St. Domingo and Laura* was published in 2007. His work has appeared in *ALH, Modern Language Studies,* and *Messy Beginnings: Postcoloniality and Early American Studies* (2003). Together, Drexler and White are writing a book entitled *The Traumatic Colonel,* which uses the figure of Aaron Burr to describe the structures of fantasy that animated early American republicanism.

KATHERINE FAULL is Professor of German and Humanities and Chair of the Department of Foreign Language Programs at Bucknell University. She has published articles on Schleiermacher and feminist theory, Moravian theology and gender, produced a translation and edition of Moravian women's memoirs, and edited two volumes on the German Enlightenment notions of race and gender, and most recently on translation and culture. She is currently completing a volume on Moravian pastoral care in the eighteenth century and another edited volume on masculinity and religion. Her newest project focuses on cultural interaction and transmission between Native Americans and Europeans in Colonial America.

PHILIP GOULD is Professor of English at Brown University. His most recent book is *Barbaric Traffic: Commerce and Antislavery in the Eighteenth-Century Atlantic World* (2003). With Vincent Carretta he is editor of

"Genius in Bondage": *A Critical Anthology of the Literature of the Early Black Atlantic* (2001).

APRIL LANGLEY is Associate Professor of English at the University of Missouri-Columbia. She has published essays on eighteenth-century black authors Lucy Terry, Phillis Wheatley, and Olaudah Equiano. Her book entitled *The Black Aesthetic Unbound: Theorizing the Dilemma of Eighteenth-Century African American Literature* was published in 2008.

ROBERT S. LEVINE is Professor of English at the University of Maryland, College Park. He is the author of *Conspiracy and Romance* (1989), *Martin Delany, Frederick Douglass, and the Politics of Representative Identity* (1997), and *Dislocating Race and Nation* (2008), and the editor of several volumes, including *Martin R. Delany: A Documentary Reader* (2003) and *The Norton Anthology of American Literature, 1820–1865,* 7th edition (2007).

PHILLIP M. RICHARDS is Professor of English at Colgate University in Hamilton, New York. His scholarship, literary criticism, and journalism have been published in a number of professional journals and magazines. He is the author of *Black Heart: The Moral Life of Recent African American Letters* (2005).

JOHN SAILLANT is currently professor in the Departments of English and History at Western Michigan University. He teaches courses in African American studies, early American history, American religion, and American literature. All his degrees were earned at Brown University and he held fellowships or postdoctoral positions at Harvard University and the Massachusetts Institute of Technology before moving to Michigan. He continues to write on early American racial ideology.

XIOMARA SANTAMARINA is Associate Professor of English at University of Michigan. She is the author of *Belabored Professions: Narratives of African American Working Womanhood* (2006).

ED WHITE is Associate Professor of English at University of Florida. He is the author of *The Backcountry and the City: Colonization and Conflict in*

Early America (2005), and various articles on the literary genres of colonization, early American nationalism, conspiracy theory, and problems of early U.S. literary history. His essays have appeared in *ALH, PMLA, American Literature, American Quarterly,* and *College Literature.*

Index

Index

PS 153 .N5 B49 2008

Beyond Douglass
191763235

TE DU